11- 2000

What the Bible Says

MIRACLES

DOUGLAS CONNELLY

InterVarsity Press
Downers Grove, Illinois

InterVarsity Press® is the book-publishing division of InterVarsity Christian Fellowship®, a student movement active on campus at hundreds of universities, colleges and schools of nursing in the United States of America, and a member movement of the International Fellowship of Evangelical Students. For information about local and regional activities, write Public Relations Dept., InterVarsity Christian Fellowship, 6400 Schroeder Rd., P.O. Box 7895, Madison, WI 53707-7895.

Cover illustration: Roberta Polfus

ISBN 0-8308-1959-2

Printed in the United States of America ∞

Library of Congress Cataloging-in-Publication Data

Connelly, Douglas, 1949-
    Miracles: what the Bible says/Douglas Connelly.
        p.   cm.
    Includes bibliographical references and indexes.
    ISBN 0-8308-1959-2 (alk. paper)
    1. Miracles.   I. Title.
BT97.2.C66   1997
231.7'3—dc20   96-43161
                                                                 CIP

20   19   18   17   16   15   14   13   12   11   10   9   8   7   6   5   4   3   2   1

13   12   11   10   09   08   07   06   05   04   03   02   01   00   99   98   97

To our daughter, Kim,
and our son-in-law, Mike

Acknowledgments		*9*
Chapter 1	SEARCHING FOR A SIGN	*11*
Chapter 2	SHOULD WE EXPECT MIRACLES TODAY?	*22*
Chapter 3	WONDERS IN THE NATURAL WORLD	*38*
Chapter 4	VICTORY OVER DEATH	*50*
Chapter 5	REBUKING THE DEVIL	*62*
Chapter 6	WHY WE GET SICK	*79*
Chapter 7	WHAT TO DO WHEN YOU GET SICK	*90*
Chapter 8	"DO YOU HAVE ENOUGH FAITH?"	*105*
Chapter 9	MIRACLES OF DECEPTION	*115*
Chapter 10	WAITING FOR A MIRACLE	*126*

Appendix 1: Biblical Nature Miracles   *139*
Appendix 2: Miracles of Judgment   *142*
Appendix 3: Miracles of Jesus   *144*
Notes   *148*
Scripture Index   *152*
Subject Index   *155*

Acknowledgments

I've dedicated this book to our daughter and her husband. Karen and I prayed for Kim's mate even before she met Mike, and we continue to ask God to bless their marriage and their new life together.

Eight men enrich my life with their support and encouragement: Steve Aikman and Tom Skaff hold me accountable and share their lives with me; Rich Tesner, Bill Sobey, Matt Johnson, Ken Gilbert, Ernie Eckerdt and Dick Adomat pray for me as Promise Keepers and as friends.

Cindy Bunch-Hotaling, my editor at IVP, does a great job and always finds time to listen to my ideas and to share hers with me. Jan Lund deserves a special thanks too for her hard work at the word processor during a difficult time in her life.

My greatest encouragement comes from my wonderful wife, Karen. She keeps my perspective on the right things and warms my heart with her tender love. My parents, Paul and Mary, and my sons, Kevin and Kyle, bring lots of joy and put up with my distractedness.

I thank God, too, for the marvelous congregation I am privileged to serve. The people of Cross Church touch my life deeply with their love and sacrifice. I never feel more safe than when I am surrounded by these friends.

Chapter 1

SEARCHING FOR A SIGN

*N*o one expected tiny Kasey Flory to survive. She was born four months premature and at birth weighed only fifteen ounces. The nurses who helped with the delivery told Kasey's father to take a good look at her because she probably wouldn't make it to the end of the hall. When Kasey did survive to the end of the hall and beyond, the doctors tried to prepare her parents for the worst: she could be blind or deaf or mentally disabled—or all three.

Two days later her weight had dropped to twelve ounces. In her first months of life Kasey endured heart surgery, spinal taps, blood transfusions and ninety-two days in a hospital incubator. But to everyone's amazement, she survived. Today Kasey is an energetic high-school student. Her mother calls her "a miracle child from God."[1]

Terry Mocny answered a knock on the door one night to be told by a police officer that his son Ed was being taken to the hospital after a severe car accident just a few miles from home. The impact of the crash shattered the first cervical vertebrae in Ed's neck and separated his skull from his spine. Physicians at the University of Michigan Medical Center in Ann Arbor told Ed's family that injuries like his were almost always fatal or resulted in permanent paralysis.

Sixty-four days after the crash, Ed Mocny walked out of the hospital with virtually no lingering effects from his injury. The twenty-one-year-old college student was dubbed "the miracle boy" by the staff at the hospital. Ed and his family give the credit for his remarkable recovery to the Lord. "Miracles do happen," Ed said. "I'm living proof of that."[2]

A Centreville, Virginia, family was making plans for a funeral. Tommy Cram, their seventeen-year-old son, had survived the surgical removal of a tumor in his brain, but now the cancer had spread to his spine. Doctors tried chemotherapy, but Tommy asked to have the treatment stopped after enduring several bouts of intense sickness from the drugs. The doctors gave Tommy absolutely no hope—he could expect to live only one to eight months. Five months later, however, routine tests to track the progress of the cancer produced astonishing news. The x-rays showed no sign of the tumor that was supposed to end Tommy Cram's life. The cancer specialist at Duke University classified Tommy's condition as remission; his parents call it a miracle.[3]

Most of us could use a miracle. Some physical condition or relational problem or financial crisis could be solved quickly with just one miracle. As we read or hear stories like the ones above, we may find ourselves wishing that God would do something supernatural for us. The Bible intensifies our desire for a miracle. In its pages we find astonishing stories of God's power poured out on people just like us.

So what exactly is a miracle—and should we expect miracles in our lives? What can we do to experience God's power unleashed in the struggles and problems we face every day? This book will attempt to answer those questions clearly and practically. Our primary source of information, however, will not be the stories of seemingly miraculous events that can be gleaned from newspapers or inspirational magazines. We will look instead at the Bible to discover what God says about miracles and then try to apply what we learn to the issues we face in our lives today. I will share some astonishing accounts of miraculous things God has done. But what will give us hope and assurance of God's care and his ability to work powerfully in our lives is not the experiences of other people but the promises of God himself.

I hope you are ready to stand in amazement at God's ability to work in powerful ways, because you will witness some awesome events. I also hope that you are ready to restructure aspects of your own life, for what you learn will prompt you to pray differently, to face pain and loss differently and to see God differently than ever before.

Focusing on the Supernatural
Christians are not the only ones looking for a miracle. Our culture is consumed with an intense interest in the supernatural. *A Course in Miracles* has sold more than one million copies since its publication in 1975. The three-volume set was supposedly "dictated" to psychologist Helen Schucman over a seven-year period (1965-1972) by a "voice" that claimed to be Jesus. The "miracles" promised by the *Course* are not supernatural events like the miracles of the Bible but are the restructuring of a person's mind. The *Course* leads people to accept a mix of New Age and Hindu beliefs while putting off the "evil" beliefs of Christianity.

The early pages make clear that the miracles discussed in the course are simply indoctrination into unbiblical deceptions. These were the words first dictated to Schucman: "This is a course in miracles. It is a required course. . . . Miracles are everyone's right . . . miracles to heal the sick and raise the dead because you made sickness and death yourself, and can therefore abolish both. . . . This is a course in mind training."[4]

Even though *A Course in Miracles* is not really about miracles, it holds out the promise of wonderful changes in hearts and minds and circumstances. In reality the *Course* leads away from Christ and not closer to him. Dean Halverson, in his careful evaluation of the *Course,* concludes that "the good news of the *Course,* upon closer inspection, turns bitter. . . . The Jesus of the *Course* is not the Jesus of the Bible."[5]

The prospect of physical healing has also captured the attention of our society. Deepak Chopra made the transition from a leader in the Transcendental Meditation movement to the head of the mind-body medicine division of a prestigious southern California hospital. Now he is a widely recognized author and lecturer on the spiritual aspects of physical healing. "Nature is man's healer" is Chopra's confident declaration.

What Deepak Chopra actually promotes are ancient Hindu principles known as Ayurveda. According to these principles, miracles of healing do not come from the hand of God but are examples of "the spontaneous remission of disease." New Age healing techniques are closer to magic than to miracle. Chopra has become nothing more than a pagan shaman to a sophisticated secular society that desperately seeks some way to overcome the relentless drumbeat of the aging process.[6]

The search for the miraculous has permeated Christianity as well. Some of the fastest-growing segments of evangelical Christianity are those that hold out the promise of supernatural financial success or physical healing or a restored marriage.

Within the Roman Catholic Church, a renewed emphasis on the elevation of worthy people to the level of sainthood has sent patrons in search of miracles that can be directly attributed to the prospective saint. Without clearly attested miracles confirmed by the church's investigators, the campaign for sainthood is virtually lost. Saints and miracles have been intimately connected for centuries. After Louis of Anjou, the young bishop of Toulouse, France, died in 1297, witnesses testified to sixty-six miraculous cures, including twelve people raised from the dead. More recently Pope John XXIII, who died in 1965, already has more than twenty miracles of healing credited to his intercession.[7]

Mary, the mother of Jesus, has reportedly appeared more than twenty-one thousand times since her death. In 1208 Mary is said to have given St. Dominic the prayer beads known as the rosary. In 1326 Mary told a farmer where to find a carved image of herself that had been buried for more than six hundred years. The statue transformed Guadalupe, Spain, into a major shrine. In 1981 Mary was seen by some young people in Medjugorje, Yugoslavia (present-day Bosnia-Herzegovina). The visions continued for years. Although the Catholic Church has not approved or authenticated the apparitions, millions of pilgrims have converted the tiny village into a major center of devotion to Mary.

What does the Bible say about such apparently supernatural events? Should we expect miracles today? If so, how can we know they are from God? A first step toward a biblical perspective on the issue of miracles is to take a careful look at Scripture to see how the mighty works of God's power are described.

Defining the Miraculous

We use the word *miracle* in a variety of ways. Every student has uttered those apprehensive words "If I pass this test, it will be a miracle!" We call it a miracle if we narrowly avoid a car accident

15

or if someone survives a plane crash. But, if we want to discover how God has worked in miraculous ways in the past and what our expectations should be about miracles today, we need to examine carefully the basic words used in Scripture to describe miracles: *sign, wonder* and *power.* Each carries significant meaning, and, when we combine the three words, we gain significant insight into why and how God works in miraculous ways.

Sign. Occasionally the biblical writers use the word *sign* to refer to ordinary events: circumcision was a sign of Abraham's faith (Romans 4:11); the observance of the sabbath was a sign of God's covenant relationship with Israel (Exodus 31:13); even the strips of cloth in which the infant Jesus was wrapped were a sign to the shepherds of who he was (Luke 2:12). The word is most often used, however, to refer to a supernatural event, a miraculous work of God with special meaning.

The apostle John selected seven miracles of Jesus to write about in his Gospel, and he called them "signs" (see appendix 3). For instance, Jesus healed a man who had been born blind (John 9:1-16); he turned water into wine (John 2:7-11); he even raised Lazarus from the dead (John 11:43-48). All were signs, supernatural events designed by God to point to Jesus as the Messiah promised to Israel.

When God sent Moses to Egypt to lead the people of Israel out of bondage, Moses asked God to give him a sign to prove that he had really sent him. God gave him three signs, three miracles designed to point out Moses as God's true representative: Moses' rod turned into a serpent; his hand turned leprous; and water from the Nile would turn to blood (Exodus 4:1-9). These signs were given to Moses "so that [the people of Israel] may believe that the LORD, the God of their fathers . . . has appeared to you" (v. 5). When Moses performed these confirming signs before the people of Israel, the people were convinced that God had sent him (vv. 30-31).

The plagues God sent on the land of Egypt were also signs—signs that the Lord was in fact the true God (Exodus 7:3, 17) and that the descendants of Jacob were in fact the Lord's chosen people (Exodus 3:10). Moses' testimony forty years later was "The LORD brought us out of Egypt with a mighty hand and an outstretched arm, with great terror and with miraculous signs and wonders" (Deuteronomy 26:8).

The reluctant warrior Gideon asked the angel of the Lord for a sign that would confirm God's message. The offering he prepared was consumed by fire springing miraculously from the rock on which it was laid (Judges 6:16-22). When the apostle Paul wanted to defend his authority as a true representative of Christ, he reminded the Corinthian Christians that "the things that mark an apostle—signs, wonders and miracles—were done among you" (2 Corinthians 12:12).

God's miracles always have a purpose. They are not done to entertain, nor does God simply act on a whim. Miracles are signs; they point to God's message or messenger as the real thing.

Wonder. God's miracles are always amazing. Called wonders, they produce astonishment in those who experience them or hear about them. When Jesus set a man free who had been possessed by demons, the man went throughout the region of Decapolis broadcasting what Jesus had done for him. Everyone who heard his story was amazed (Mark 5:20).

Genuine miracles from God arouse a response of wonder and awe and even fear in peoples' minds. On one occasion Jesus was asleep in the back of a boat when a furious storm began to rage. In a panic the disciples woke him up. Jesus rebuked the wind and the waves, and instantly the tempest stopped. In Matthew's account we are told that the men were amazed (8:27); Mark says that the men were afraid (4:41); Luke writes that *"in fear and amazement* they asked one another, 'Who is this? He commands even the winds and the water, and they obey him' " (8:25).

Miracles make us catch our breath or drop our jaws; we listen and look in astonishment. When God does a miraculous work, the appropriate response is to wonder and marvel at what he has done.

Mighty work. Miracles are also acts that demonstrate God's power. No human being is ever given the credit for a genuine miracle. God may, and often does, use human beings as the visible channel through which the miracle comes, but the miracle is always clearly a work of divine power. Jesus' miracles were works of power (Matthew 11:20; 13:58); the resurrection of Jesus from the dead was a miraculous evidence of God's power (Romans 1:4; Philippians 3:10); even Jesus' conception in Mary was accomplished by the "power of the Most High" (Luke 1:35); God created the earth by his power (Jeremiah 10:12). Miracles are supernatural works, events that can be explained in only one way—God did this!

A combination of these words is often used in Scripture to refer to a period of intense miraculous activity. Moses reminded the people of Israel that "before our eyes the LORD sent *miraculous signs and wonders*—great and terrible—upon Egypt and Pharaoh and his whole household" (Deuteronomy 6:22; see also Exodus 7:3; Psalm 135:9). The apostles in the early church "performed many *miraculous signs and wonders*" (Acts 5:12; see also Acts 4:30). Peter pointed out the significance of Jesus' miracles: "Jesus of Nazareth was a man accredited by God to you by miracles [literally, mighty works], wonders and signs" (Acts 2:22). As the apostles began proclaiming the gospel, their message was confirmed by "signs, wonders, and various miracles [mighty works]" (Hebrews 2:4; see also 2 Corinthians 12:12).

The biblical definition of a *miracle*, then, is "an unusual, amazing event (wonder) that is clearly a work of supernatural power (mighty work) and that is designed to point out something significant that God is doing (sign)."

The Father's Care

It is extremely important that we make a distinction in our minds between God's work through *miracles* and God's work through his *providence.* God normally works in our world and in our lives through his providence; that is, he governs and preserves our universe according to predictable patterns. Hebrews 1:3 tells us that God the Son is continually "sustaining all things by his powerful word." God is actively involved in our world but in a way we do not sense directly. The seasons come and go; rain falls; the rotation of the earth continues—all are evidences of God's sustaining work of providence.

We have made spectacular progress in science and technology in the last one hundred years precisely because God has made and continues to maintain a universe that acts in a predictable way. We observe nations rising and falling, and historians point out the political, economic and social reasons for such events, but behind the scenes "the Most High is sovereign over the kingdoms of men and gives them to anyone he wishes" (Daniel 4:17; see also Job 12:23; Psalm 22:28). God has a purpose and plan for the events that take place in our world, but normally he accomplishes that purpose by standing in the shadows and working through secondary causes.

When God works miraculously, he steps out of the shadows and intervenes directly in a particular situation. Under God's *providential* care, we may recover from a sickness because we take the proper medication (which works in a predictable way) and because we rest and nourish our bodies in a way that (predictably) brings recovery. When God heals someone *miraculously,* one (or all) of these elements are removed. God may heal instantly without the need for rest and the passage of time. God may heal over time but without medication or surgery. God steps in directly and works above the normal, predictable laws of nature to bring about his desired result.

What I want to emphasize is that in *both* situations God is actively at work. God is just as much involved in a gradual, providential recovery as he is in an instantaneous, miraculous healing. God simply chooses to work in different ways depending on his desired purpose. God may also allow the "natural" order of things to bring about death. Several years ago my wife, Karen, and I watched her mother slowly die from congestive heart disease. As difficult as that process was, what gave us confidence and peace was that God was involved in the process with us. He was not absent; he had not abandoned his child. God did not miraculously intervene, but he was still personally present and lovingly involved.

"It Was a Miracle"

I have explained God's providence because we need to make a clear distinction between God's normal providential care in our lives and God's unusual miraculous intervention. At the beginning of this chapter I told you about three people who experienced spectacular recoveries from illness or injury. As apparently "miraculous" as those stories sound, all three were actually works of God's providence. In each case, medical treatment and time for recovery were required. Sometimes a lingering complication remained. God's power certainly was evident in each person's survival and recovery, but God still worked through secondary means instead of through direct miraculous intervention.

Maybe a personal illustration will help make the distinction clear. I was talking one day to a woman in our church, and we happened to be standing at the top of a long flight of stairs. As we talked a small child was making his way up the steps. When he reached the top, he let go of the stair rail and suddenly began to totter dangerously backward. I was paralyzed for a second, but the woman reacted instantly. She grabbed the front of his bibbed overalls just as he began to fall. Her quick action saved that little boy from a serious fall.

The response was to comment on what a "miracle" it was that we happened to be standing precisely at that spot and that she was able to react so quickly. But from what we have seen in Scripture, what happened was not a miracle. It demonstrated God's remarkable care for this child, but it was a work of God's *providence*. God saw to it through the normal ordering of events that we were standing at the right place at the right time. God prompted the woman's "radar" to see what was happening and to respond quickly. God may even have kept me from responding because if both of us had tried to grab him, we might have gotten tangled up and missed the child. No angel miraculously intervened (at least that we could see or sense). Instead, God worked through secondary means to accomplish what he desired.

As we look at miracles in the Bible, and particularly as we seek to discover how God may choose to work miraculously in our lives today, we need to keep this distinction between God's normal providential care and God's less frequent direct miraculous intervention in mind. God *is* actively involved in all that we do, even if we do not see a miracle in our lives. Even the normal, predictable, routine, "vanilla" events are ordered by a sovereign God. We are not alone. We dwell "in the shelter of the Most High" and "rest in the shadow of the Almighty" (Psalm 91:1). We can even "give thanks in *all* circumstances" (1 Thessalonians 5:18) because in the shadows of our lives stands a loving heavenly Father and we are in his hands. He cares for us deeply; he sustains us constantly; he is able to do in us and through us and for us more than we can ever think or imagine.

Chapter 2
SHOULD WE
EXPECT
MIRACLES
TODAY?

*W*hen you pick up the Bible, it seems as if miracles appear on every other page: a great sea divides, city walls fall down, sick people are instantly healed, water is turned into wine. All are demonstrations of God's mighty power. But if you read the Bible carefully, you find that intense miraculous activity occurred in only four periods of biblical history. In between those relatively short periods are long epochs in which very few miracles occurred. The four clusters of intense miraculous activity are easy to identify.

The first came during the time of Israel's escape from Egypt and the conquest of the Promised Land. In this span of about fifty years, from God's call to Moses at the burning bush to Joshua's victories in Canaan, God's people saw more miracles than anyone had in the tens of thousands of years since creation.

The devastating plagues on Egypt, the miraculous deliverance at the Red Sea, the provision of manna in the wilderness, bitter water made sweet, healing from poisonous snake bites and the collapse of the walls of Jericho were just a few of the wondrous works of God that marked this exciting period in Israel's experience.

After the conquest of Canaan, a long period of time ensued in which miracles occurred infrequently. Hundreds of years passed—the time of the judges, the glorious days of David's kingdom, the whole reign of great king Solomon—in which very little miraculous activity was recorded. God had not left his people alone; he was still actively involved in directing and instructing them through the written Law and his spokespersons, the prophets. But few miracles are recorded. No one (at least as far as we can tell from the biblical record) lamented the absence of miracles as evidence that God did not care for his people or that God was weak or even that his people lacked sufficient faith for miracles to occur. There seems to be no expectation or demand for God to intervene miraculously, even in times of great crisis in the nation or in people's lives. What characterized this time was a confident trust in the Lord to rule in his kingdom as he desired.

The second period of intense miraculous activity centered around the ministries of Elijah and Elisha, two of God's prophets to the northern kingdom of Israel. After Solomon's death, his son, Rehoboam, acted foolishly toward the clans that made up the northern section of the nation. Consequently, those clans split off from the ruling clans of Benjamin and Judah in the south. The northern kingdom quickly strayed spiritually from the Lord. Apostasy and idolatry began to gain wide acceptance, from the king's palace on down. This idolatrous worship of pagan gods reached its climax in the reign of Ahab and his Phoenician wife, Jezebel (1 Kings 16:29-33).

As a warning to Israel, God raised up a courageous prophet, Elijah, who prayed fervently that God would keep his promise of judgment. God had told the people centuries earlier that if they departed from wholehearted obedience to God and his law, God would send chastening upon them. One method of reproof that God specifically mentioned was the withholding of rain from the land (Deuteronomy 11:16-17). Elijah asked God to keep his word, then went to King Ahab and announced that there would be no rain until he as God's prophet said there would be. Three years of dreadful drought followed Elijah's announcement.

Finally, Elijah challenged Ahab and the prophets of the Phoenician god of the storm to a contest on Mount Carmel. An altar would be built, a sacrifice would be placed on the altar, prayers would be made, and the god who answered with fire to consume the sacrifice would be declared the true God of Israel. When the prophets of Baal prayed, nothing happened; but when Elijah spoke one simple prayer, God answered with a blast that consumed the sacrifice, the wood, the stones of the altar and the gallons of water poured over the sacrifice.

In the years that followed, Elijah was used by God to perform many works of power. The same miraculous element marked the ministry of Elijah's successor, Elisha. These men were even used by God to raise back to life two young boys who had died.

The people of the northern kingdom were certainly not seeking the Lord during this time of great miracles. They were not people of faith. The majority had abandoned the Lord and were following after the gods of the nations around them. Furthermore, after Elisha's death the nation once again entered a period in which very few miracles occurred. Through the next several hundred years, almost no miracles are recorded in either the northern or southern kingdoms. Several prophets followed Elijah and Elisha, both in the north and the south, but most of them were never instruments of anything miraculous. God was with his people; he had not left them alone. Even in times of disobedience, God was faithful to his promises. God spoke to Isaiah and Jeremiah and Hosea, and they gave the people God's message. But very few, if any, miraculous works of power marked their ministries.

It was not until the days of Israel's captivity in Babylon that miracles once again were seen in abundance. Daniel and his three close friends were taken to Babylon in 605 B.C. Under constant pressure to compromise their faith and commitment to the Lord, these men stood firm—and they saw miraculous deliverance from every attempt to discredit or destroy them. Some of the most spectacular of God's miracles in the Old Testament took place during the life and ministry of Daniel in Babylon.

Shadrach, Meshach and Abednego, Daniel's faithful friends, were saved from death in the fiery furnace. Daniel was delivered from the lions' den without a scratch—not because the lions weren't hungry but because an angel closed the lions' mouths. A man's hand mysteriously appeared in Belshazzar's palace and wrote the final epitaph over the crumbling Babylonian empire. God was demonstrating his continued care and active involvement with his people even when they were under God's chastening hand in a place far from the land of God's promise.

But after Daniel's death, miracles again ceased. In the time of Esther (480-460 B.C.), God once again delivered his people from an evil effort to destroy them, but this time God did it through works of his providence. He worked behind the scenes through ordinary events and people to bring about the results he desired.

The church I am privileged to pastor recently decided to enter into a building program. To give us some perspective on the challenges that lie ahead of us, I am planning to preach a series of messages from the Old Testament book of Nehemiah, the story of the rebuilding of the wall of the city of Jerusalem after the time of Israel's captivity. What I have noticed in my study of the book is that no miracle takes place anywhere in the story. God is certainly involved in all that goes on. He moves the king's heart to give Nehemiah permission to return to Jerusalem and rebuild the city; he gives Nehemiah a plan that will galvanize the people and bring them together to work; God thwarts the attempts of Nehemiah's enemies to compromise the work; and the resulting success is clearly the evidence of God's good hand on his people. But nowhere is there a miracle! No angel appears; the walls do not instantly rise up from the rubble around the city. The whole exciting story takes place during a time when God chose not to intervene in human history with miraculous works of power.

The only clear departure from this pattern of miracles being clustered around a few key periods of time are miracles of judgment. God intervenes miraculously several times in the Old Testament to bring destruction on individuals or groups even when other miracles are virtually absent (see appendix 2). The destruction produced by the flood in Noah's day was clearly a miraculous act of God's judgment (Genesis 6:5-7; 8:21). During Abraham's lifetime Sodom and Gomorrah were destroyed by direct divine intervention (Genesis 19:14-26), though the closest thing to a miracle that Abraham experienced was the conception in Sarah of a child (Genesis 21:2). Uzziah, one of Judah's kings, was instantly struck with leprosy when he attempted to take the place of the priest in the temple of God (2 Chronicles 26:19-21). Later, King Hezekiah and the prophet Isaiah prayed fervently for God's protection from the Assyrian army, and one angel destroyed 186,000 Assyrians in one night (2 Chronicles 32:20-22; Isaiah 37:36).

Five hundred years passed between the time of miracles in

Daniel's day and the fourth period of biblical miracles. An incredible amount of literature was written during this time by the Jews, but these writings confirm that it was a time marked by few miracles. When Jesus began his ministry, God's people once again saw a remarkable outpouring of miracles. In fact, the miraculous activity surrounding Jesus' three-and-a-half-year ministry far overshadows anything anyone had seen before (see appendix 3). Jesus virtually eliminated sickness from Galilee during the height of his ministry. Sick people were brought to him by the hundreds, and he healed them all. Blind people were given sight; crippled people were made whole; thousands of hungry people were fed by miraculous provision. Jesus' works of power brought even his enemies to the point of wonder and awe.

This fourth period of biblical miracles extended beyond Jesus' earthly ministry into the early years of the church. Peter and John, two of Jesus' apostles, healed a crippled man who was sitting at one of the gates of the temple. In fact, for a while the apostles continued to have a ministry of miracles similar in scope and power to Jesus' own ministry. Luke the historian writes, "The apostles performed many miraculous signs and wonders among the people. . . . Crowds gathered also from the towns around Jerusalem, bringing their sick and those tormented by evil spirits, and *all of them* were healed" (Acts 5:12, 16).

A few years later, Philip, one of the deacons in the Jerusalem church and an effective evangelist, went to the region of Samaria and began to preach the gospel. Healings and the casting out of demons accompanied Philip's ministry (Acts 8:6-7). The apostle Peter was released from Herod's imprisonment by the miraculous intervention of an angel (Acts 12:1-19). The apostle Paul healed a crippled man in Lystra (Acts 14:8-10); he cast a demon out of a slave girl (Acts 16:16-18);

he shook a poisonous viper from his hand with "no ill effects" (Acts 28:3-5); and he healed Publius, the chief official of Malta, and others on the island who were sick (Acts 28:7-10). The most intense time of miraculous activity in Paul's ministry apparently was in Ephesus during his second church-planting journey: "God did extraordinary miracles through Paul, so that even handkerchiefs and aprons that had touched him were taken to the sick, and their illnesses were cured and the evil spirits left them" (Acts 19:11-12).

Miracles Diminish
Although miracles occur throughout the book of Acts, two facts become clear. First, the number and frequency of miracles do not approach the level of miraculous activity during Jesus' ministry. Second, as you read Acts and the New Testament letters, you will notice some hints that the intensity of miracles began to decline during the seventy years following Jesus' resurrection. In what is probably the earliest New Testament letter, James tells those Christians who are sick to call the elders of the church for anointing and prayer (James 5:14-16). James does not urge believers to seek out a healer or even to look for another Christian with the gift of healing. The matter is to be handled quietly within the context of the local church.

In the letter of Galatians, written early in Paul's ministry, Paul talks about his suffering from a physical illness: "As you know, it was because of an illness that I first preached the gospel to you. Even though my illness was a trial to you, you did not treat me with contempt or scorn. Instead, you welcomed me as if I were an angel of God, as if I were Christ Jesus himself" (Galatians 4:13-14). No one knows for sure what Paul's illness was precisely,[1] but the point is that Paul was sick and was not miraculously healed.

In another one of Paul's letters, the apostle talks several times about gifts of healings and gifts of miracles that were opera-tive in the church (1 Corinthians 12:9, 28, 30). But in 2 Corinthians, written a few years later, Paul says that he was suffering from "a thorn in [the] flesh"—apparently a physical affliction that God allowed to continue in Paul's life to keep him from becoming conceited because of the wonderful revelations he had received (2 Corinthians 12:7-9). Paul even pleaded with the Lord to remove the thorn, but God gave him grace to endure the affliction rather than granting a miraculous cure.

In his letter to the Philippians, a book written near the end of the events recorded in Acts, Paul tells us about Epaphroditus, a faithful servant of Christ, who became deathly sick in Rome (Philippians 2:25-30). Though Paul could not heal him, God did ultimately bring Epaphroditus back to health, but not through a miraculous healing.

The young pastor Timothy suffered from "frequent ill-nesses," including a troubling stomach disorder (1 Timothy 5:23). Paul counsels him to use wine in moderation to calm his stomach. Paul did not say, "I'll heal you," or "Find a healer"; he told him to take some medicine.

In Paul's final letter, written just before his death, we read these words: "Erastus stayed in Corinth, and I left Trophimus sick in Miletus" (2 Timothy 4:20). Paul uses the same Greek word here to describe Trophimus's illness that he used in referring to Epaphroditus's near fatal sickness.

The contrast is remarkable! At the beginning of the book of Acts, multitudes are being healed; at the end of New Testament history, the companions of the apostles have to be left behind because of serious illness. The New Testament writers do not express regret that the intensity of spectacular miracles had begun to decrease. The apostles do not chastise individuals or churches for their lack of faith. They simply recognize that this period of abundant miraculous works was ending.

So What About Today?

Based on the pattern of miraculous activity seen in the Bible, I believe that we are living in a time marked by few miracles. We are in one of those long time spans when spectacular miracles are not part of God's program.[2] That does not mean that God has abandoned us. Nor does it mean that we are less blessed or loved by God. God still works powerfully in our lives and in human history to accomplish his desires. He simply works by means of his providence, through events and people, rather than directly through miracles.

We are not to grieve over the absence of miracles but rejoice in God's faithfulness. As a pastor, I am not called to rebuke my congregation for their lack of faith if God does not heal someone miraculously. I am called to help those in my congregation to walk by faith and to remind them that God's love and care never diminish, even when the storm seems strongest and the night seems darkest.

I do not want you to think that I rule out miracles completely. I *do* believe that God continues to work miraculously in our lives, but he works through what I call "family miracles." The miracles in the time of Jesus' ministry and the early days of the church were spectacular and public. Today, almost two thousand years later, God works quietly and compassionately in response to the prayers of his children.

Carol Sintay, a vibrant young woman in our congregation, was diagnosed with extensive cancer. Several doctors had seen the tumor on the ultrasound screen and had felt the tumor with their trained hands. The doctors urged Carol to have immediate surgery even though it interrupted a master's degree program she was enrolled in. A few days before the surgery, Carol asked the elders to anoint her and to pray for the Lord's healing. In obedience to the pattern of James 5, we willingly agreed. When the surgeons operated, they found no tumor and no traces of the cancer. Carol had been healed—powerfully and miraculously. It was not by her power or by our power as elders or by the doctors' power. The healing was accomplished by God's power alone in response to the obedient, humble cries of his children. God's people responded with awe and wonder—and praise to God.

On the other hand, I have seen men and women die from cancer who were just as faithful to Christ as was Carol and who had just as much faith in the Lord and were just as obedient. A lovely, gracious woman in another congregation I pastored developed a brain tumor. She asked God to heal her; the elders anointed her and prayed fervently. In a few months her mind and body had degenerated to the point where she could hardly move. A few days later she died. In God's wise plan, he chose to heal this dear woman in a different way—he took her into the presence of Christ.

But Didn't Jesus Say That His Followers Would Perform Greater Miracles Than He Did?
In a recent article in our local newspaper, a pastor addressed the issue of whether we should expect miracles today by appealing to Jesus' words in John 14:11-12:

> Believe me when I say that I am in the Father and the Father is in me; or at least believe on the evidence of the miracles themselves. I tell you the truth, anyone who has faith in me will do what I have been doing. He will do even greater things than these, because I am going to the Father.

Based on this passage, that pastor contended that we Christians should expect to see the same outpouring of miracles that Jesus saw in his ministry and even greater evidences of God's power. But is that what Jesus meant? If it *is* what he meant, shouldn't we see an increase in the number of miracles as we read through the book of Acts and on through the rest of the New Testament? Why don't we read of the apostles' doing more miraculous works than Jesus did—or greater works—or at least the same number of works? What we find, however, is a gradual decline in the frequency and number of miracles. The writers of the New Testament never seem surprised by that; they never admonish the church for its lack of miracles or for its lack of faith.

I believe that the apostles knew that the number of miracles would gradually decline. As the New Testament writings became available and as the gospel became established in the Roman world, spectacular, public miracles occurred less and less. Even inside the church, we read of very few miracles toward the end of the New Testament age. In the age that followed the New Testament, miracles almost completely cease.[3] But no church father grieves over the fact that the period of miraculous activity has come to a close. No early father accuses the church of failing to pursue the greater works that Jesus promised they would do. All this leads me to believe that Jesus had something different in mind when he said that the apostles and those who came later would do greater works than the ones Jesus himself did.

As wonderful and as powerful as Jesus' miracles were, they met only a temporary need in people's lives. The sick people Jesus healed and the disabled people Jesus made physically whole eventually died. Hungry people who were fed by the miraculous multiplication of a few fish and loaves of bread became hungry again. Lazarus, who was raised from the dead at the spoken word of Christ, died a second time. The Sea of Galilee that became calm at Jesus' word has been rocked by many storms since then.

However, as the apostles went out to the nations with the

message of the gospel, they saw eternal changes take place. People who were lost in sin found forgiveness and cleansing in Christ. Men and women who were far from God and who were excluded from the covenants and promises of God to Israel were drawn near to God by the blood of the cross. Those who believed in Christ were made new creatures; the old life passed away and the new life began. These were the "greater works" Jesus spoke of, because the miracle of salvation met humanity's deepest need and met that need permanently and eternally.

Since Jesus' death, resurrection and ascension, many apostles, pastors, missionaries and laypeople have led more people to saving faith than the Son of God did in his entire ministry—and these evangelizing Christians have done it without one miracle. I am convinced that these "greater works" of reaching lost men and women with the gospel are God's basic program for the church until Christ returns. We should see "power evangelism" at work as we who know Christ present the gospel, because the gospel is "the *power* of God for the salvation of everyone who believes" (Romans 1:16).

Why Back Then and Not Today?
I make it a practice after our Sunday-evening services to have a few minutes for open questions from the congregation. We have followed some interesting biblical "rabbit trails" together. One Sunday evening several years ago, after I had presented my perspective on the pattern of miracles in the Bible and my view on miracles today, a young college student asked a perceptive question: "If dramatic miracles are part of God's program for such a limited time, why have miracles at all?" I gave a rather brief answer that night, but I have thought about the question a lot since then. The Bible gives four clear reasons for miracles in God's plan.

First and foremost, *supernatural signs were intended to con-*

firm certain messengers and their messages as sent and approved by God. When Moses was commissioned by the Lord to go to Egypt as the instrument of Israel's release from bondage, Moses raised an important issue: "What if they do not believe me or listen to me and say, 'The LORD did not appear to you'?" (Exodus 4:1). In other words, how can I convince these people that I didn't just suffer sunstroke out here in the desert and dream all this stuff up? How will they know that the Lord really sent me?

In response to Moses' question, God gave Moses three sign miracles to perform as confirmation that he was a spokesperson for the Lord: his staff became a snake when thrown to the ground, his hand became leprous when placed inside his cloak, and water from the Nile would become blood when it was poured on dry ground (Exodus 4:2-9).

When the prophet Elijah burst on the scene to confront Ahab and the people of Israel with their abandonment of the true God, God again gave sign miracles as confirming evidence of Elijah's divine mission. The miracles of Elijah and Elisha established the office of prophet as God's megaphone to his people. A few prophets had ministered before the time of Elijah and Elisha and many prophets came after them, but the authority of the prophets was confirmed by the miraculous signs performed through these two men.

In the time of Daniel, God's people again were in a life-and-death situation. The tiny remnant of the nation had been carried off in captivity to Babylon. But when they arrived God already had positioned men in places of influence in the Babylonian government. Daniel and his friends were miraculously delivered from death not simply to impress their captors with the Lord's power but also to assure God's people of his continuing love and care for them in a foreign land.

The miracles that Jesus performed were not done just to help hurting people. Jesus *was* moved with compassion for human suffering, but his miracles were much more significant than mere acts of kindness. Jesus' miracles marked him out as the Anointed One of God, as Israel's promised Messiah. Nicodemus, a member of Israel's ruling council, recognized the meaning of Jesus' miracles: "No one could perform the miraculous signs you are doing if God were not with him" (John 3:2). When Peter stood up at the Feast of Pentecost to proclaim the gospel, he said, "Men of Israel, listen to this: Jesus of Nazareth was a man accredited by God to you by miracles, wonders and signs, which God did among you through him" (Acts 2:22).

As John the Baptist sat in Herod's prison, he began to question whether Jesus really was the Messiah. When John's disciples brought the question to Jesus, Jesus turned to a gathering crowd and healed many of those who were sick and blind and lame. Then Jesus told John's followers to return to John and report what they had seen. The Old Testament declarations that the Messiah would come with confirming miracles was being fulfilled before their eyes (Matthew 11:2-4; see also Isaiah 35:5-6).

The miracles of the apostles and others in the early church had the same effect. The miracles confirmed their words as a true message from God. When Philip preached the message of Christ in Samaria, the historian Luke adds this analysis of what happened: "When the crowds heard Philip and *saw the miraculous signs he did,* they all paid close attention to what he said" (Acts 8:6). But the clearest explanation of the importance of miraculous works in the early church is found in Hebrews 2:3-4:

> This salvation, which was first announced by the Lord, was confirmed to us by those who heard him. God also testified to it by signs, wonders and various miracles, and gifts of the Holy Spirit distributed according to his will.

God added his divine stamp of approval to the preaching of the gospel by giving signs, wonders, various miracles, and gifts of the Holy Spirit.

However, just as in other periods of intense miraculous activity in Scripture, once God's message was announced and confirmed by miracles, the confirming miracles gradually decreased in number and frequency. As the gospel message and God's directives for this age came to be written down under the Spirit's guidance, the need for confirming miracles diminished. There are certainly other purposes for miracles, but this one seems to be of primary importance. Miracles authenticated God's messengers and God's message at crucial times in the history of God's people.

A second purpose of miracles is to demonstrate God's power and to draw people to believe God's truth. The apostle John carefully selected seven sign miracles as the framework for his Gospel. He chose those seven out of the hundreds of miracles Jesus performed because he thought those particular signs would bring the reader of his Gospel to "believe that Jesus is the Christ, the Son of God" (John 20:30-31). Peter's miraculous healing of Aeneas, a paralytic, caused those who saw the healed man to turn to the Lord (Acts 9:32-35). When Tabitha was raised from the dead, it "became known all over Joppa, and many people believed in the Lord" (Acts 9:36-42). Miracles alone will not bring people to faith (the *gospel* is the power of God to salvation), but when the gospel was first proclaimed, God testified to its truth with miraculous works to draw people to faith.

Another purpose of miracles is to help people who are in need. As Jesus went to a small village one day, he was met by the funeral procession of a widow's only son. "When the Lord saw her, his heart went out to her" (Luke 7:13). Jesus was often moved with compassion and pity for people who were suffering (see, for example, Matthew 9:36; 14:14; 20:30-

34). So he raised her son to life.

Finally, *miracles bring glory to God.* Everything God does is designed to display his glory and majesty. After Jesus forgave a paralytic and confirmed his authority to forgive sins by healing the man's body, the crowds who saw it "were filled with awe; and they praised God, who had given such authority to men" (Matthew 9:8). Every miraculous work of God should produce in us a sense of wonder that prompts expressions of praise and adoration to him.

Chapter 3
WONDERS IN THE NATURAL WORLD

*W*hat a sight on the capital parade grounds! Every major and minor government bureaucrat stood in uniform for a widely publicized show of loyalty to the nation's dictator. These showcase political events were so well orchestrated that they usually went off without a hitch. After a few speeches, everyone went home. But today things were different. All eyes were on three newcomers—foreigners, no less—who had chosen to defy the state ruler over some personal religious technicality. How had these men ever made it into the civil bureaucracy in the first place?

Whatever their religious qualms, the three had chosen the wrong day to make their point. The general was in a foul mood. They had spoiled his party. There was no formal arrest and no trial: execution was immediate as a warning to all. The method of execution on this occasion was particularly sadistic, even for a particularly cruel leader. An old smelting furnace near the parade grounds was fired up to white-hot heat. The men would be tied up, carried out on the catwalk above the furnace and thrown in alive.

The general had a seat where he could see every second of their torture. The furnace was so hot that several state security agents collapsed as they carried the men toward their certain death. The three men did not even seem to struggle—but fanatics often faced death unafraid. The general watched the spectacle with glee and then with shock. It was hard to see clearly, but it looked like the three men were walking around in the furnace talking to a fourth man who did not look like a man at all. He looked like a son of one of the gods!

Finally the old general found his voice and called the men out. His aides thought he had lost his mind, but the three men walked out of the furnace. They were unharmed and untied. The only things that had burned up in the fire were the ropes that had bound them. The evil empire was never the same after that day.

That story really happened. You did not read about it in the newspaper because it happened twenty-five hundred years ago. Hananiah, Mishael and Azariah—better known to us as Shadrach, Meshach and Abednego—refused to bow in worship to the image crafted in reverence to Nebuchadnezzar, the Babylonian king. Their preservation in the fiery furnace recorded in Daniel 3 is one of the best-known and most dramatic miracles in the Bible.

In fact, events such as the protection of these three men in the fire are what usually come to mind when we think of miracles. Several times in the pages of the Bible we are confronted with powerful stories of God's intervention in human history. God overrides the normal predictability of our world in dramatic events that we call miracles.

We see these marvelous works of power bursting through what we consider the normal and predictable routine of life in each of the eras of biblical history marked by intense miraculous activity. In the days of Israel's exodus from Egypt, God opened the Red Sea and allowed his people to escape from Pharaoh's pursuing army (Exodus 14:21-22). Normally, bodies of water do not open to allow large groups of people to walk across on dry ground. A few summers ago, when I stepped into the Atlantic Ocean off the coast of Delaware, the water simply closed in around my feet. The farther I walked from shore, the higher the water rose around me. That is what water predictably does. But at a crucial moment in Israel's history, when it seemed that the entire nation would perish, God powerfully intervened to make a way of escape. The dividing of the Red Sea and the subsequent destruction of Pharaoh's army became the defining example of God's great power for hundreds of years. Whenever a writer of Scripture in the Old Testament wanted to point to the one miracle that demonstrated the awesome ability of Israel's God to save his people, he pointed to the deliverance of Israel at the Red Sea (Psalms 66:5-6; 106:9; 136:10-15; Isaiah 51:10; 63:11-13).

During the forty years following the exodus, several other wonders in the natural world took place: manna fell from heaven to feed hundreds of thousands of Israelites (Exodus 16); water gushed from a rock to quench their thirst (Exodus 17); the fortified walls of Jericho fell down (Joshua 6); and the sun seemed to stand still in the sky so that Israel's enemies could be routed (Joshua 10).

In the days of Elijah and Elisha, fire came from heaven to consume a soggy sacrifice and to prove that the Lord alone was God (1 Kings 18:19-39). Meal and oil were miraculously provided to keep Elijah, a widow and the widow's son alive through a famine (1 Kings 17:7-16). We normally expect that an iron axhead that fell into a river would sink to the bottom; in response to Elisha's prayer, however, God made an axhead float (2 Kings 6:1-6).

Nature miracles were part of Jesus' ministry too. Twice Jesus fed thousands of people by multiplying a few loaves of bread and a couple of small fish (Matthew 14:15-20; 15:32-38). Under normal circumstances, two things are required to make wine—grapes and time. Jesus' first miracle was the immediate transformation of gallons of water into exquisite wine (John 2:1-11). In the middle of a raging storm on the sea of Galilee, Jesus walked on the surface of the water to the boat where his disciples were struggling to survive (Mark 6:47-51). At Jesus' shout of command, the wind and turbulence of a mighty storm were brought to perfect calm (Luke 8:22-25).

Did Jesus Really Walk on Water?
These wonders in the natural world are the most spectacular of the Bible's miracles. They are also the hardest miracles for our rational minds to believe—and they are the easiest miracles for the skeptics to attack. Critics of the Bible often contend that the miracle stories we read in Scripture grew up around the memory of well-known biblical characters long after they had died. When the early church began to grow (the critics claim), the Gospel writers needed to spice up the story of Jesus in order to enhance his image among his new followers. So the writers added popular pious stories to make Jesus out to be more than a humble carpenter and gentle teacher. Since his birth was relatively uneventful, the authors of the Gospels added the spectacle of a miraculous virgin birth. Although Jesus may have had some reputation as a healer, the Gospel writers tried to portray him healing multitudes of sick people in the most spectacular way. Most skeptics of the Bible dismiss the miracle

accounts by claiming that the writers of Scripture simply incorporated later legends and folk stories into the biblical account.

Other skeptics try to explain or rationalize the miracle accounts. I once read an article in which the author tried to argue that, as the Israelite army marched around the city of Jericho, the rhythmic beat of the army's feet sent vibrations into the earth that triggered an earthquake. The walls fell down, but it was not because of God's miraculous intervention, just the fortunate shifting of the earth's crust. Some critical commentators on the Gospels suggest that when Jesus "walked" on the water, he was in reality walking on a sandbar that stretched out into the Sea of Galilee. From Jesus' vantage point on the hillside above the sea, he could see the sandbar and was concerned that his disciples would run aground, so he walked out to warn them of their imminent danger. Later, as the disciples told the story, they said that Jesus had walked on the water to the boat.

How do we know that these spectacular nature miracles really happened? I'm not going to give you a full-blown defense of biblical miracles,[1] but I think a few points will help assure you that we can put full confidence in the reliability of the biblical record.

First, *the historical records of Jesus' miracles and teaching have been demonstrated to be absolutely reliable.* The Gospels were written by men who were actually with Jesus or were close associates of those men. Even the critics of the Bible have to admit that every strand of the Gospel record contains accounts of miraculous events. All the Gospel writers and all the "sources" for the Gospel accounts that the scholars have "uncovered" are filled with stories of Jesus' miracles. As the critical scholars try to unravel the various threads of legend and history that they claim were woven together to create the Gospel accounts, they are forced to admit that the miraculous aspect of Jesus' ministry permeates every layer.

Jesus' miracles can't be easily dismissed even by those who deny the trustworthiness of the Bible.

Second, *Jesus himself taught that miracles were a crucial element in his ministry as Israel's Messiah* (Matthew 11:2-6; 12:28; John 10:25). Even the enemies of Jesus acknowledged the reality of his miracles. His opponents accused him of working by Satan's power instead of by God's, but they never questioned the miracles themselves (Matthew 12:24; Mark 3:30; Luke 11:14-16). The apostle Peter stood before thousands of people and said that Jesus had been accredited by God by means of "miracles, wonders and signs"—then he added, "as you yourselves know" (Acts 2:22). The people listening to Peter had witnessed Jesus' miracles. If the miracles had never really happened, they could have (and *would* have) rejected everything Peter said. Instead, three thousand of those who listened put their personal faith in Jesus and publicly identified themselves as his followers (Acts 2:41). The evidence for Jesus' miracles is as good as or better than the evidence for any historical event or person in the ancient world.[2]

Many respected scholars have demonstrated that the Gospel accounts give us an accurate picture of what Jesus did and said—and that leads to the third foundation for our belief in miracles: *because we can trust the Gospels, we can rely on* Jesus' *testimony when it comes to the miracles recorded in the Old Testament.* Jesus consistently assumes that the miracles of the Old Testament actually took place. In fact, Jesus deliberately puts his stamp of authenticity on the miracles most often rejected by the skeptics: Adam and Eve were real people (Matthew 19:3-6); the great flood actually occurred (Luke 17:26-27); the city of Sodom was destroyed by God (Luke 17:28-29); God spoke to Moses from the burning bush (Luke 20:37); manna supernaturally sustained the people of Israel in the wilderness (John 6:49); Elijah's prayers resulted in a famine in Israel (Luke 4:25); the leper Naaman was healed after following Elisha's instructions (Luke 4:27); and Jonah was actually swallowed by a huge fish (Matthew 12:40).

When I was a college student, in one of my classes I raised the issue of Jesus' testimony to the reality of a man named Jonah and the historicity of Jonah's experiences in the fish. The professor looked at me with the special pity he reserved for those he sensed were "religiously naive." He then explained that if Jesus really made the statement about Jonah in Matthew 12:40 (a fact he sincerely doubted), Jesus was merely accommodating his language to the beliefs of the people who heard him. First-century Jews actually believed the story of Jonah, and Jesus did not want to offend them. When I pointed out that his view made Jesus a liar, he ended the discussion by shouting, "Grow up, Mr. Connelly!"

This unbelieving professor is not the only person who has suggested that Jesus merely accommodated himself to the popular beliefs of his day. I spoke on Jonah a few years ago at a summer Bible conference in western Michigan. I made the point in my opening message that Jesus taught that Jonah was a real person who really was swallowed by a fish. A woman came up after the service and said that she thought my approach to the Jonah "fable" was very naive. She further explained that Jesus had simply played along with this story because everyone believed it and Jesus hadn't wanted to offend his listeners. I responded by pointing out that Jesus never hesitated on any other occasion to point out false belief, so why would he hesitate at this point? Furthermore, since God raised Jesus from the dead and by that act of power declared Jesus to be the Son of God, can't we conclude that God was also putting his mark of authenticity on everything Jesus had done and said?

The biblical accounts of miracles are either lies, legends or history. C. S. Lewis summed up the issues a little differently in his book *Mere Christianity:* Jesus was either a liar, a lunatic or Lord of all.[3]

Spectacular Miracles Today

Most of us Christians do not need to be persuaded that the biblical miracles were real events. We believe in a personal God who is actively involved in our lives and who is able to do whatever he purposes to do. God's miraculous intervention in our world is not something we struggle with. The question we struggle with is "Should we expect to see the same kinds of miracles that we read about in the Bible in our lives today?"

I have already given you part of my answer drawn from the pattern of miraculous activity in the Bible. The spectacular wonders that seem to fill the Bible are actually confined to a few periods of intense miraculous outpouring designed to authenticate a new messenger or message from God. We are living today in one of those long interludes in which we see few dramatic, public miracles. We are called to walk by faith, not by sight.

But I can hear objections to that position. One is "Aren't you limiting God? If you say that God won't intervene miraculously in our world, aren't you putting God in a box?" My answer is no. I hope nothing I say or write ever gives anyone the impression that I have figured out what God will or will not do. God is absolutely free; he is not limited or confined by anything—except his own character and his own Word. I believe we are living in an age *not* marked by spectacular miracles because that is the pattern I see clearly set down in Scripture. Relatively short periods of intense miraculous activity are followed by very long periods of very few miracles. Does God work miraculously today? Absolutely! But he does it quietly within the confines of the believing family.

I realize that some Christians will disagree with me sharply on this issue. Rapidly growing segments of the evangelical community believe that God will work today in the same spectacular ways he did in the early church if we as Christians simply open ourselves to God's power. They believe that evangelism, for example, should be marked by dramatic evidences of God's victory over demons or sickness or even death. "Power evangelism" would transform the entire work of world evangelization.

While those who advocate wondrous works of power have many stories to tell of miracles, the number and wonder of their accounts do not compare with the widespread miraculous activity that surrounded the ministry of Jesus or the early church. Those who proclaim that the same level of miraculous power is available today have to abandon the biblical pattern of periods of intense miracles followed by long periods of relative inactivity. Our age, they claim, is different from earlier times. Jesus "intended" that we would work miracles today. Their biblical support for that position, however, seems weak.[4]

As a young theologian, the great church father Augustine (354-430) believed that miracles were necessary in Jesus' day to persuade people that Jesus was the Messiah. Miracles ended with the apostles, he said, so that believers would not seek merely visible assurance for their faith and because miracles, by becoming customary, would no longer be wondrous. Later in life Augustine clarified his position and said that he did not mean that no miracles would occur but that they would be fewer and less public than Jesus' miracles. As a faithful pastor to the Christians in Hippo, a city in Roman North Africa, Augustine had seen many miracles that God had given to comfort and encourage his people.[5]

Moving Mountains
"But didn't Jesus say that if we had enough faith we could move

mountains?" Yes—and he said it would take faith only the size of a tiny mustard seed to do it (Matthew 17:20). On another occasion Jesus spoke a word of judgment on a fig tree, and the tree withered. When the disciples saw what happened, they asked exactly what we would have asked: "How did the fig tree wither so quickly?" Jesus gave a profoundly moving answer:

If you have faith and do not doubt, not only can you do what was done to the fig tree, but also you can say to this mountain, "Go, throw yourself into the sea," and it will be done. If you believe, you will receive whatever you ask for in prayer. (Matthew 21:21-22)

If we believers have enough faith or if the church as a whole would be stirred to believe in miracles, shouldn't we see the same great dramatic works of God in our world today?

I admit that these verses are powerful statements from Jesus, but I am not convinced that he was talking about moving a literal Pike's Peak! Jesus makes his statement about faith and moving mountains in the context of the disciples' failure to cast out a demon from a young boy (Matthew 17:14-16). When the disciples ask why they could not drive the demon out, Jesus tells them that it is because they have so little faith. Then he adds the statement about moving the mountain. Jesus is using a figure of speech to talk about how his disciples were to overcome hindrances to the work of extending God's kingdom. I do not think those men went away determined to rearrange the geography of Palestine. Instead, they were forced to see (just as we are forced to see by Jesus' dramatic words) that success in the work of God is not linked to technique or training but to confident, humble reliance on God alone.

One Sunday after I had preached on these verses, a woman came up to me and said, "You are part of the reason we *don't* see miracles today. You teach people not to believe in miracles, and so the whole church is shrouded in unbelief. If miracles would return, we would see the world brought to Christ overnight!" She then reminded me of Jesus' unwillingness to perform miracles in his own hometown of Nazareth because of the unbelief of the people (Mark 6:5-6). Her words prompted me to look openly and prayerfully at what I believed and at what I had taught my congregation. The last thing I wanted to do was to cultivate a spirit of unbelief.

I concluded that my position did not promote unbelief at all. No one talked more about trusting in God's wisdom and power alone than I did—and no one tried harder to model faith than I did. But part of faith is to learn God's ways and to trust him even when we cannot see the path ahead. Genuine faith holds tightly to its confidence in God's wisdom and love even when the miracle does not come in our lives.

I was even more skeptical about the woman's statement that a return of spectacular miracles would prompt millions to believe in Christ. When Jesus healed multitudes of sick people and fed thousands by multiplying one boy's sack lunch, many believed but many others still refused. Hardhearted Pharisees and greedy religious leaders saw astonishing works of power with their own eyes, then plotted to kill the man through whom the miracles came. Jesus himself said that if unbelievers will not be drawn to saving faith by the testimony of God's Word, they will not be persuaded by someone who miraculously comes back from the dead either (Luke 16:31).

An Unfailing Vitamin Bottle

Spectacular miracles in the natural world may be limited by God to certain times in his program for human history, but his active care for his people is continuous. Corrie ten Boom in her classic story of faith *The Hiding Place*[6] gives a remarkable account of God's astonishing care for her in the Ravensbruck concentration camp. Corrie had been able to bring a small bottle of vitamin drops into the camp barracks. She gave her sister, Betsie, a drop each day, hoping that the vitamins would revive her sister's failing health. Corrie tried to hoard the drops, but soon other women crowded around to get a drop. "It was hard to say no," she writes, "to eyes that burned with fever, hands that shook with chill. I tried to save it for the very weakest—but even these soon numbered fifteen, twenty, twenty-five . . . and still, every time I tilted the little bottle, a drop appeared at the tip of the glass stopper."

Betsie reminded Corrie of the story in the Bible about the widow in the town of Zarephath, who in faith fed the prophet Elijah before feeding herself and her son with the last bit of her food. From that day on, through the whole time of famine and drought, "there was food every day for Elijah and for the woman and her family. For the jar of flour was not used up and the jug of oil did not run dry" (1 Kings 17:15-16). Corrie tried to find a rational explanation; Betsie simply accepted it as "a surprise from a Father who loves you."

Several weeks later another prisoner brought Corrie a small cloth sack filled with vitamin pills. She was elated with the treasure and decided to finish the drops before using the pills. "But that night, no matter how long I held [the bottle of drops] upside down, or how hard I shook it, not another drop appeared."[7]

God could have miraculously flattened the barbed-wire perimeter of the camp and allowed the prisoners to escape. God could have sent an angel to slay the guards so that the prisoners would have had enough food. All the options were within God's power, but he chose to demonstrate his unfailing care by quietly multiplying vitamin drops until other provisions were made. I hope you respond to Corrie ten Boom's story with wonder and praise to God. If you do, you have begun to grasp the purpose for God's miraculous works.

Chapter 4
VICTORY
OVER
DEATH

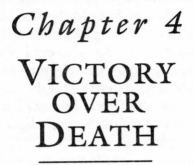

*F*rank Morison was convinced that the Gospels were unreliable witnesses to Jesus. Furthermore, his study of physics left him dogmatically opposed to the reality of Jesus' miracles. Although he had a high regard for Jesus as a wise and good teacher, this young student was convinced that "miracles do not happen." From that perspective, Morison decided to write a book on what he considered to be the most important phase of Jesus' life—the days leading up to the crucifixion. His goal was to strip away from the gospel story all the overgrowth of church dogma and speculation so that his readers could see Jesus as the supremely great and noble person that he was.

As Morison pursued his research, however, he was forced more and more by the evidence he uncovered to change his mind. His study of Jesus' death and the claims for Jesus' resurrection landed him, he says, "on an unexpected shore."[1] Frank Morison was gradually persuaded that a miracle *had* occurred—Jesus had risen from the dead. More important than his intellectual conversion was his spiritual conversion. Morison put his faith not simply in a good man but in the Lord of glory.

Morison wrote his book—not the book he had intended to write but a book presenting the evidence he had uncovered and the struggle that the evidence had sparked in his own mind and heart. For decades *Who Moved the Stone?* has been a stirring defense of the reality of Christ's victory over death.

Several miracles in the Bible center on death. A few people don't have to go through it; quite a few return from it; and one person goes beyond it!

Enoch and Elijah were taken directly to heaven without experiencing physical death. In Genesis 5, the narrator of the book gives us a long list of those patriarchs who lived and died before the great flood. It's about as exciting to read as a ten-year-old obituary column—until you come to the verses about a man named Enoch.

Enoch was born, lived, fathered sons and daughters (including Methuselah, whom a girl in our Sunday school identified as "the longest liver in the Bible"). But unlike all the others in the list, Enoch did not die. "Enoch walked with God; then he was no more, because God took him away" (Genesis 5:24). The New Testament author of Hebrews points to Enoch as a man of faith: "By faith Enoch was taken from this life, so that he did not experience death; he could not be found, because God had taken him away. For before he was taken, he was commended as one who pleased God" (Hebrews 11:5). I wish we were told more about Enoch and his journey to heaven, but that's all we have. I think it significant that Enoch's transport into heaven is the only miracle recorded in Scripture in the long span of time from creation to the flood.

The prophet Elijah went to heaven in a whirlwind stirred up by a chariot of fire and horses of fire. At the end of Elijah's ministry, God prompted him to take his companion, Elisha, and to walk into the wilderness east of the Jordan River. As they walked "suddenly a chariot of fire and horses of fire appeared and separated the two of them, and Elijah went up to heaven in a whirlwind" (2 Kings 2:11). We are never told why God chose such a dramatic way to bring Elijah's earthly ministry to an end. By contrast, his faithful friend, Elisha, simply died and was buried (2 Kings 13:20). The great lawgiver, Moses, the servant of the Lord, died, and God buried his body (Deuteronomy 34:5-6). Even men such as Abraham, the friend of God, and David, the man whose heart was joined with God, simply died. They were "gathered to [their] people" (Genesis 25:8; see 1 Kings 2:10). Many of God's servants suffered torture or execution, and no miracle rescued them. But Enoch and Elijah never felt that last sting of death.

A whole generation of Christians will have the same experience of being taken to heaven without death. The apostle Paul tells us that when Christ returns for his church, not only will all the dead in Christ be resurrected, but "we who are still alive and are left will be caught up together with them in the clouds to meet the Lord in the air. And so we will be with the Lord forever" (1 Thessalonians 4:17). Your name may never be listed in the obituary page, and my funeral service may never be held! *We* may be the believers who are alive when Christ returns and who are "raptured" into his presence without facing death. That wonderful possibility should motivate us to joyful, godly living even in difficult circumstances. We are not trying to find ultimate fulfillment in this life; we are waiting for God's Son from heaven—"Jesus, who rescues us from the coming wrath" (1 Thessalonians 1:10).

"Lazarus, Come Out!"

Even though the prophet Elisha died and was buried instead of being taken directly to heaven, one of the strangest events in the Bible centers on Elisha's bones. Many years after Elisha's death, the people of Israel were under attack from marauding Moabites. Some Israelites who were digging a grave to bury the body of a friend of theirs saw a Moabite raiding party heading toward them and panicked. Instead of taking time to dig a grave, they rolled back the stone on the nearest tomb (which happened to be Elisha's) and rather unceremoniously tossed their friend's body inside. What happened next was not what they expected: "When the body touched Elisha's bones, the man came to life and stood up on his feet" (2 Kings 13:20-21).

In the pages of the Bible, eight people (including this man) were raised miraculously back to life after death. Elijah and Elisha each raised a child to life (1 Kings 17:19-24; 2 Kings 4:32-37). Jesus raised three people who had died during his ministry: Jairus's daughter (Matthew 9:18-19, 23-25), the son of the widow in the city of Nain (Luke 7:11-15) and Jesus' friend Lazarus (John 11:1-44). The apostle Peter raised Dorcas back to life (Acts 9:36-42), and the apostle Paul raised Eutychus, a young man who fell asleep during a sermon and then fell from a third-story window to his death (Acts 20:7-12).

The people who witnessed these mighty acts of power responded exactly as people are supposed to respond to God's miraculous works: Jairus and his wife were "completely astonished" (Mark 5:42); the people attending the funeral in the village of Nain were all "filled with awe and praised God" (Luke 7:16). These miracles functioned as "signs" too. As a result of the raising of the dead boy in Nain, the people began to announce, "A great prophet has appeared among us. . . . God has come to help his people" (v. 16). Following the raising of Lazarus, "many of the Jews who had come to visit Mary, and had seen what Jesus did, put their faith in him" (John 11:45). The enemies of Jesus responded to the miracle too—not by putting their faith in him but by plotting to kill Jesus *and* Lazarus (John 11:57; 12:10-11).

Two general observations can be made about these miracles of restoration to life. First, in several of the miracles, some strange actions were used to bring the miracle about. Jesus raised Jairus's daughter simply by taking her hand and saying, "Little girl, I say to you, get up!" (Mark 5:41). When the grave of Lazarus was opened, Jesus spoke just one command, "Lazarus, come out!" (John 11:43), and Lazarus emerged alive.

When Peter was brought to the room where Dorcas's body was laid, he "got down on his knees and prayed." Then he spoke a quiet command: "Tabitha [her name in Aramaic], get up." She opened her eyes and sat up, and Peter took her hand and helped her to her feet (Acts 9:40-41). When Paul raised Eutychus, the procedure was a little more complex. Paul went outside the building in which he had been speaking to the place where Eutychus had fallen. He "threw himself on the young man and put his arms around him." Then he announced to the gathered believers, "Don't be alarmed. . . . He's alive!" (Acts 20:10).

Paul may have based his action on the example of Elijah, who, after laying the dead son of the widow of Zarephath on the bed and praying, "stretched himself out on the boy three times" and cried, "O LORD my God, let this boy's life return to him!" (1 Kings 17:21). In the case of Elijah's prophetic successor, Elisha, a boy returned to life after the prophet prayed and then "lay upon the boy, mouth to mouth, eyes to eyes, hands to hands." When Elisha did it the second time, "the boy sneezed seven times and opened his eyes" (2 Kings 4:34-35). We are not told why God directed his prophets to use such unusual methods, but it is emphatically clear that God, not the methods and not the prophets, restored life to these boys.

My second observation about the biblical miracles of reviving to life centers on how modern-day skeptics approach these accounts. They simply dismiss as untrue the miracles in the natural world, such as walking on water or multiplying bread, but their approach to miracles of raising the dead is to explain the miracle away.

Several years ago I sat through a ninety-minute lecture by a prominent theologian during which he tried to persuade us that Lazarus had not died but only lapsed into a coma. Jesus wept at Lazarus's tomb (we were told) not because of the devastating pain brought upon human beings by sin and death, but because the people of Bethany were not medically advanced enough to detect the coma and Jesus was fearful that Lazarus had suffocated in the tomb! But when the stone sealing the tomb was removed, allowing a blast of fresh air to sweep over Lazarus, and when Jesus awakened him with a shout, Lazarus revived. Later, the author of John's Gospel jazzed up the story by making it appear that Jesus had raised the dead when in fact he had only rescued his friend from premature burial. The lecturer ended by expressing his hope that his explanation of John would attract rational people "back to Jesus." Instead, people left more disillusioned than ever.

In every account of a miraculous reviving, clear testimony is given that the person had died. Lazarus had been dead four days. Dorcas's body had been washed and laid out for burial. Eutychus (according to Luke the physician, who witnessed the event) was "picked up dead." If you read the Gospel accounts of Jesus and Jairus's daughter, you might conclude that she was one, at least, who had not really died, for Jesus said, "The girl is not dead but asleep" (Matthew 9:24; the same remark is repeated in Mark 5:39 and Luke 8:52). But Luke points out that when Jesus told the girl to get up, "her spirit returned," and she stood up (Luke 8:55).

The Bible's definition of physical death is the separation of the body and the spirit (James 2:26). The body is buried; the spirit lives on in consciousness, either in a place of blessing or in a place of torment. In all eight biblical instances of restoration to life, the spirit of the person was reunited with the body, and the person returned to life.[2] By saying that the girl was asleep, Jesus was not denying her death; he was emphasizing the temporary nature of her condition. Among the Jews and Christians who believed in the resurrection of the dead, the expression "asleep" was a common way of referring to the temporary state of death (see 1 Corinthians 15:1-28; 1 Thessalonians 4:14-17).

Jesus made the same point in relation to Lazarus: "Our friend Lazarus has fallen asleep; but I am going there to wake him up." The disciples thought that Jesus meant literal sleep, but John added this explanation: "Jesus had been speaking of his *death*, but his disciples thought he meant natural sleep." So Jesus "told them plainly, 'Lazarus is dead' " (John 11:11-14).

Resurrection Ahead

I wish we knew what Lazarus experienced during his four days in the grave. But not one of these people in the Bible who were restored to life ever says anything about what they saw or heard or felt. They did not work the talk-show circuit or sign lucrative book contracts. In fact, one tragic reality marks all those who were raised from the dead—they were returned back to this earthly life and had to die again.

One of the Bible's back-from-the-dead accounts, however, is different from all the others. Jesus died and was buried and rose again. But he was not simply revived; he was resurrected. He did not return to this earthly life in a body plagued by thirst or hunger or weakness or pain. He was raised to a whole new life in a glorified human body. Lazarus revived to die again; Jesus is alive and will *never* die again. Jesus walked into the jaws of death and conquered that final enemy. He stands beyond death and beyond the grave not as the victim of death's cruel attack but as the victor over death forever.

As powerful as the miracles of reviving to life are, the resurrection of Jesus far surpasses those miracles in its awesomeness and majesty. The prominent miracle in the Old Testament, the miracle every writer pointed to as the supreme example of God's mighty power, was God's opening of the Red Sea and Israel's deliverance from the Egyptian onslaught. In the New Testament, the supreme miracle is the resurrection of Jesus. When the apostle Paul, for example, wanted to point out the awesome ability of God to work in the lives of Christians, he reminded his readers that God's power "is like the working of his mighty strength, which he exerted in Christ when he raised him from the dead and seated him at his right hand" (Ephesians 1:19-20).

"Declared with Power to Be the Son of God"

Not only is Jesus' resurrection the most remarkable miracle in the Bible, it is also the bedrock foundation of the Christian faith. Christianity without the resurrection is not Christianity at all. Two crucial facts about Jesus are confirmed by his resurrection from the dead.

First, the resurrection demonstrates the approval of God the Father on all that Jesus said and did. Peter, speaking for all the apostles, declared on the Day of Pentecost, "[Jesus] was not abandoned to the grave, nor did his body see decay. God has raised this Jesus to life" (Acts 2:31-32).

Second, the resurrection confirms Jesus' own claims to deity. Paul almost shouts as he opens his letter to the Romans that Jesus "was declared with power to be the Son of God by his resurrection from the dead" (Romans 1:4). Jesus claimed to speak with the authority of God; Jesus claimed to act in the power of God; Jesus did things that only God could claim the right to do; Jesus gave titles to himself that only God could rightfully claim. Jesus acted during his ministry as if he stood and spoke in the place of God himself. Was Jesus really who he claimed to be—or was he insane? The resurrection proves beyond all doubt that Jesus was exactly who he said he was— God the Son in human flesh.

Jesus' resurrection also has some profound implications for those who believe in him as Savior and Lord. The resurrection assures us, for example, that the penalty and price of our sin were fully paid. On the cross Jesus died in our place, but his resurrection broke the power that sin and death and hell held over us. Our salvation is won by the complete event of Jesus' death and his victorious resurrection. Paul makes it clear that Jesus "was delivered over to death for our sins and was raised to life for our justification" (Romans 4:25). The gospel message is not just that "Christ died for our sins" but also that "he was raised on the third day" (1 Corinthians 15:1-4). Any presentation of the gospel that doesn't include the resurrection is incomplete; faith in a Jesus who is still in the grave is in vain, empty of power to save.

The miraculous resurrection of Jesus also gives us great assurance in the face of death. The sting of death has been removed, and for the believer death means falling asleep in Jesus. His triumphant victory is the guarantee of our future resurrection. Our weak, sinful bodies will be changed to be like Christ's glorious body (Philippians 3:21). The resurrection will complete the process of transformation into the image of Christ that has been the Father's goal in each of our lives (Romans 8:29). On that day, our physical and psychological healing will be complete. We will be revealed as the glorious beings God created us to be.

The Bible also assures us that the resurrection of Jesus is the foundation of our belief that Jesus will personally return in glory. The expectation of the Second Coming of Christ permeates the New Testament. Christians for almost two thousand years have eagerly looked for Christ's literal, physical return, and we base that hope on the literal, physical resurrection of Jesus from the dead. Paul said it best: "We believe that Jesus died and rose again and so we believe that God will bring with Jesus those who have fallen asleep in him. . . . For the Lord himself will come down from heaven with a loud command, with the voice of the archangel and with the trumpet call of God" (1 Thessalonians 4:14, 16).

"Even If Someone Rises from the Dead"
Our resurrection as believers is future—but what about today? Should we expect to see miracles of revival to life? A few reports of people being raised to life have surfaced in the past twenty years or so, but they are as rare as the revivings in the Bible. Only eight people in the whole scope of biblical history were raised to life—five of them within the few decades shared by Jesus and the apostles Peter and Paul.

When a believer in Christ dies, the spirit of that believer goes to be with Christ (2 Corinthians 5:8). We may miss that person deeply, and the separation may be sudden and painful, but why would we want to bring that person back? The Bible says that to depart and to be with Christ is "better *by far*" than anything we can experience in this life (Philippians 1:23). To expect or to pray for a miracle to return a believer to this life seems inconsistent with the whole emphasis of New Testament teaching.

You might be tempted to think that a miracle such as raising the dead would make a powerful impact on the unbelieving world. But I'm afraid you would be wrong. In the story Jesus told of the rich man who died and went to a place of torment, the rich man asks that a poor, dead beggar who used to sit outside his home and was now enjoying his eternal reward be sent back to warn the rich man's brothers about the place of torment. The response is sobering: "If they do not listen to Moses and the Prophets [God's written Word], they will not be convinced even if someone rises from the dead" (Luke 16:31).

The most powerful witness to Christ's power to save lost men and women is not a stupendous miracle. The most powerful witness is a clear, simple presentation of the gospel coming from a man or woman or young person who has been redeemed by the blood of Christ. It is that message that God has promised to use to draw lost people to faith in Christ. It is the *gospel* that is "the power of God for the salvation of everyone who believes" (Romans 1:16). The miracle of the new birth occurs when a man or woman hears the message of Christ's saving grace and responds in faith.

"I Am Alive Forever"

Betty Eadie, in her bestselling book *Embraced by the Light*,[3] claims to have died and returned to life four hours later. In those hours, she says, she was embraced by Jesus, given a tour of heaven and sent back to earth to finish her work. The account of the afterlife given by Eadie has been widely read and believed. But it is in direct contradiction to what the Bible says lies beyond death's door.

The near-death experiences that fill the bookstore shelves or that are shared excitedly on television talk shows do not give me much comfort when I think about my own death or the death of someone I love. How can I be sure that another person's experience is real, and how do I know if I will experience the same thing? I do not want opinion or wishful thinking or even someone else's experience when I stand at death's door. I want assurance; I want the truth.

There is *one* man who has been through the experience of death and who has come back to tell us about it—and we can trust his word completely. The man's name is Jesus. This resurrection is not based on hearsay or fable; it is not the product of wishful thinking on the part of the apostles. The resurrection is based on accurate, dependable eyewitness accounts of an empty tomb and face-to-face encounters with the risen Lord.

There's one more piece of evidence. This Jesus has met me at the deepest need of my life. By his grace he has saved me; by his power he is changing me day by day. His promise is that he will save all who come to him in faith—even *you!* I know he will save you, because he took a rebellious sinner like me and made him a beloved child of God.

Chapter 5

REBUKING
THE
DEVIL

*A*ngels are magnificent, powerful beings. They travel at incredible speeds to do their master's will. Some angels are involved in international political affairs; others are focused on the needs of children. Erase from your mind the idea that angels look like cute Precious Moments figurines. When angels appear, mere human beings are filled with fear.

The Bible has a lot of interesting things to say about angels,[1] but one truth is pressed home repeatedly. Angels are divided into two camps: the holy angels and the evil angels, angels of light and angels of darkness, angels who serve God as their Sovereign Lord and angels who serve Satan, the enemy of God. We are not told how Satan tempted other angels to follow him in his rebellion against God, but the Bible clearly teaches that a host of angels operate under Satan's authority. Jesus even referred to "the devil and *his* angels" (Matthew 25:41). These evil angels are also called demons and unclean spirits. Their work is to oppose God and his kingdom, to oppress human beings and to do the will of their master.

We do not normally think about demons when we think about miracles, but many of the miracles Jesus performed were actually miracles of liberation from demonic power. These miracles are often called exorcisms. Satan's angels are able to oppress and place people in such bondage that it requires the miraculous power of God to set them free.

Can We Really Believe in Demons Today?

Whenever I speak on evil angels and their power, someone will usually ask, "Isn't it hard in our day to believe in demons? Isn't this just the ancient explanation for mental illness?" My response is always the same. I point out that Jesus believed, acted and taught that demons were real and that they could "demonize" people in a wide variety of ways. Jesus commanded demons to leave individuals. He said that some people were deaf or unable to speak not because of a physical disability but because of demonic oppression. At times Jesus talked to demons directly.

If demons are not real, Jesus was either a deceiver or deceived himself. On the other hand, if we believe that Jesus was God with us, then we have to accept the reality of demons and their ability to oppress and at times totally dominate human beings. There are more than eighty references to demons in the New Testament. Every New Testament writer (except the author of Hebrews) refers to demons as real beings under the authority of Satan.

In our modern, sophisticated culture we may not see the wild, blatant displays of demonic influence that we encounter in the New Testament, but the same evil master is at work through his subordinates. A cultured, articulate man or woman who stands up and speaks against biblical truth is motivated by the same spirit of rebellion against God that is expressed by a pagan shaman or voodoo priestess. The apostle Paul warned that even Satan will transform himself into an angel of light if he can lead a person away from the truth that is found in Christ (2 Corinthians 11:14).

Miracles of Liberation

Overcoming the power of demons requires direct intervention from God. Even though evil angels are sinful, they still retain their power, a power much greater than our power as mere human beings. The Bible records several miracles of exorcism or liberation from demonic oppression.

The clearest miraculous victory over demonic power in the Old Testament took place on Mount Carmel when God's prophet Elijah challenged the prophets of the Phoenician god Baal to a contest. An altar was built, a sacrifice was made, prayers ascended to heaven and the deity that responded with fire was to be acknowledged as the true God (1 Kings 18:19-39). When the Lord answered Elijah's simple prayer with a megawatt blast of energy, he was not simply exposing the impotence of idols. He was also demonstrating his power over demons.

Hundreds of years before Elijah's day, Moses had reminded the people of Israel of their idolatry in the wilderness. He said that when the people made an offering to an idol, in reality they had "sacrificed to demons, which are not God" (Deuteronomy 32:17). Behind the idols and images of pagan deities stand demonic forces who use their power to deceive people into false worship (see also Psalm 106:37-38; 1 Corinthians 10:19-20).

In the New Testament, and particularly during the earthly ministry of Jesus, Satan and his demons were flushed out from under the rocks. Repeatedly in the Gospels Jesus exposes and overpowers demonic power. Sometimes the demons reveal themselves immediately; at other times they hide behind disease or deformity until Jesus rips away their mask.

Usually a person who is oppressed by a demon is said to be "demon-possessed" (Matthew 8:16; 12:22; Mark 5:15-16), but another common practice was to describe a person as "having" a demon (Matthew 11:18). Demons are said to have "gone into" a person, which made it necessary for Jesus to "drive out" the demon (Matthew 12:28; Mark 1:34; Luke 8:30). Demons "seize" some people (Luke 9:39) and "trouble" others (Luke 6:18).

An Example of Jesus' Power

In his breathlessly vivid portrait of Jesus, Mark tells us about a confrontation Jesus had with a demon-possessed man. The confrontation came in church—in the synagogue in Capernaum.

They went to Capernaum, and when the Sabbath came, Jesus went into the synagogue and began to teach. The people were amazed at his teaching, because he taught them as one who had authority, not as the teachers of the law. Just then a man in their synagogue who was possessed by an evil spirit cried out, "What do you want with us, Jesus of Nazareth? Have you come to destroy us? I know who you are—the Holy One of God!"

"Be quiet!" said Jesus sternly. "Come out of him!" The evil spirit shook the man violently and came out of him with a shriek.

The people were all so amazed that they asked each other, "What is this? A new teaching—and with authority! He even gives orders to evil spirits and they obey him." (Mark 1:21-27)

We are not told how this man happened to be in the synagogue on this particular sabbath. Did he come regularly, or did he come because he knew Jesus would be there? It's interesting (and important) that Jesus did not initiate this confrontation; the man who was "possessed by an evil spirit" (v. 23) did. Luke adds that he was "possessed by a demon, an evil [literally, unclean] spirit" (Luke 4:33). In the middle of Jesus' sermon, the man shouted out, "What do you want with us, Jesus of Nazareth? Have you come to destroy us?"

Even though the man speaks, the demon's words come out. This is characteristic of demon possession. The evil spirit or spirits so dominate a person that the demons can at times use the human being's body to express their desires. The demon's next words are shocking: "I know who you are—the Holy One of God!" The demon acknowledges that Jesus is from God. The demon knew exactly who Jesus was! Jesus was his Creator; Jesus was the Son of God. The demon even admits that Jesus would be his final Judge: "Have you come to destroy us?"

Jesus' response was immediate. He said to the demon, "Be quiet!" What the demon had said about Jesus was the truth. Jesus *was* the Holy One of God. But Jesus commanded the demon to be quiet because he didn't want unsolicited public testimony from a demon. His rebuke was stern: "Be muzzled!" Jesus' next command—"Come out of him!"—was just as forceful. The demon had no choice; he had to obey. The terror of demonic possession is displayed even in the demon's obedience to Jesus' command. The man shook violently and shrieked as the spirit left him.

The people in the synagogue were amazed at what they had witnessed. They had seen exorcists at work before, but never one like Jesus. At Jesus' word even the evil spirits obeyed. The miracle of exorcism produced in those who saw it exactly what a miracle is supposed to produce—wonder and amazement. God's power had been unleashed.

The news about Jesus spread through Capernaum like wild-fire. By evening the whole town was at Jesus' door. He healed those with diseases and "drove out many demons," but he still refused to let the demons speak (Mark 1:29-34).

The next thing Mark records in his Gospel is very instructive. After a long day of ministry to people, including healing and spiritual battle against demons, Jesus got up very early in the morning, went off to a place of solitude and prayed. Even as a Spirit-filled man, Jesus needed the renewing strength that comes from a time of solitude and communion with the Father.

Satan Driving Out Satan

Not everyone reacted to Jesus' miracles of exorcism with wonder and amazement. On another occasion some people brought to Jesus a demon-possessed man who was blind and mute. Matthew tells us that Jesus "healed [the man] so that he could both talk and see" (Matthew 12:22). The people who saw the miracle had the proper response to a display of God's mighty power—they were astonished. Jesus' enemies, however, leveled a scathing blast at the work Jesus had done. The Pharisees who hated Jesus never questioned the reality of his miracles; they questioned the source of his power. They made the blasphemous suggestion that Jesus cast out demons by Satan's power—"It is only by Beelzebub,[2] the prince of de-mons, that this fellow drives out demons" (v. 24).

Jesus responded first by pointing out how illogical their accusation was: "Every kingdom divided against itself will be ruined, and every city or household divided against itself will not stand. If Satan drives out Satan, he is divided against himself. How then can his kingdom stand?" (vv. 25-26). In effect, Jesus was saying that if Satan were working through Jesus to liberate the very people who were enslaved by Satan's power, Satan's kingdom would soon collapse.

Then Jesus turned the table on his critics. He explained that his power over demons was a distinguishing mark of his ministry. The Pharisees should have recognized Jesus' authority over demons as the confirming evidence that the long-awaited kingdom of God had begun:

If I drive out demons by the Spirit of God, then the kingdom of God has come upon you.

Or again, how can anyone enter a strong man's house and carry off his possessions unless he first ties up the strong man? Then he can rob his house. (vv. 28-29)

Satan is "the strong man" that Jesus has tied up. Jesus is probably referring to his victory over Satan's temptations in the wilderness (Matthew 4:1-11). During the rest of his earthly ministry Jesus entered the strong man's house (the world of people, including those under Satan's control) and carried off some of the strong man's possessions. Jesus liberated people from satanic bondage and brought them into the kingdom of God. The power of the Spirit working in triumph over demons was the evidence that Jesus as God's Anointed One had inaugurated the time of God's reign.[3]

Exorcism in the Early Church

Outside Jesus' personal ministry there are only a few examples of miracles of liberation from demons in the New Testament. Jesus entrusted authority over the demons to the twelve apostles as they went out to minister: "As you go, preach this message: 'The kingdom of heaven is near.' Heal the sick, raise the dead, cleanse those who have leprosy, *drive out demons*" (Matthew 10:7-8; see also Mark 3:15).

Later, seventy-two disciples were sent out two by two into every village where Jesus intended to go. When they returned to Jesus, they said in amazed joy, "Lord, even the demons submit to us in your name" (Luke 10:17). Jesus responded with this prophecy: "I saw Satan fall like lightning from heaven" (v. 18). In other words, Jesus saw in the victory of the seventy-two over demons a foreshadowing of Satan's future expulsion from heaven and confinement to the earth (see Revelation 12:7-12).

After Jesus' ascension and the powerful coming of the Holy Spirit ten days later, miracles of exorcism continued to be seen, although on a much more limited scale than during Jesus' ministry. The apostles "performed many miraculous signs and wonders" in the early months of the church's existence (Acts 5:12), including healing all who were "tormented by evil spirits" (v. 16). When Philip, the deacon and evangelist, went to Samaria to preach the message of the gospel, miraculous signs confirmed his message. Paralytics and cripples were healed, and "evil spirits came out of many" (Acts 8:5-8).

In the entire ministry of Paul only one miracle of exorcism is recorded. When Paul and Silas came to the Greek city of Philippi, a slave girl began to follow them. The girl "had a spirit by which she predicted the future" (Acts 16:16). What bothered Paul was not that the girl followed them but that she kept shouting, "These men are servants of the Most High God, who are telling you the way to be saved" (v. 17). She was speaking the truth, but Paul wasn't thrilled about the source of the commendation. Finally, after several days of this shouting, "Paul became so troubled that he turned around and said, 'In the name of Jesus Christ I command you [the demon] to come out of her!' " (v. 18). Immediately the demon left.

Paul did not use some magical incantation, nor did he have to shout or argue for hours with the demon. He simply spoke a confident word of command and appealed to the authority of Christ. The demon had no choice but to obey.

A Defeated Enemy

The New Testament writers make a powerful point that Satan and his demons have already been defeated. The spiritual war still rages around us, but the end of the story has already been written. Jesus triumphed personally over Satan in the wilderness, but Satan's decisive defeat came at the cross. Jesus came to earth as a human being so that "by his death he might destroy him who holds the power of death—that is, the devil" (Hebrews 2:14). Through Jesus' sacrificial death on the cross, God "disarmed the powers and authorities." He made "a public spectacle" of Satan's forces, "triumphing over them by the cross" (Colossians 2:15).

Furthermore, when we believe on Christ, God rescues us from the dominion of Satan's darkness and transfers us into the kingdom of his own Son (Colossians 1:13). Through personal faith in Christ, we are completely forgiven and made children in God's family. We have died in Christ to the old slave master of sin and death; we now serve a new master, Jesus Christ. The old master still tries to bark orders at us, but we have the power to refuse to follow his commands. The Holy Spirit who resides in us is far more powerful than Satan or any demon (1 John 4:4). We don't have to fear demons or Satan's attacks. The enemy has no rightful authority over us. What the apostle Paul said to the Philippian Christians about their human opponents we can also apply to our demonic enemies: "[Do not be] frightened in any way by those who oppose you" (Philippians 1:28).

If that is not enough guarantee of victory, there is one more assurance of Satan's defeat. God has told us in his Word exactly how the battle will end. After Satan has made every attempt to thwart God's redemptive plan to reclaim the universe, he will bow his knee to Jesus and will confess that Jesus is Lord (Philippians 2:9-11). Satan and his angels will then be confined to the darkness and agony of the lake of fire forever (Revelation 20:10; see also Matthew 25:41).

Dealing with Demons Today

One Sunday morning a very unusual visitor came into our church. As I walked across the foyer to greet the man, a chill ran down by back. I introduced myself and tried to carry on a conversation with him, but my mind and my spirit were repelled by his very presence. I can't explain fully why I felt the way I did except that evil seemed to radiate from him. As I walked into the auditorium to begin the worship service, I found myself deeply disturbed by this man's presence in our church. I'd never experienced anything like it before. I had welcomed skeptics, atheists, Muslims, Buddhists and plenty of plain old pagans into our services, and I had rejoiced to see them come. But this man was different.

As I sat down on the platform, I asked God to hinder any evil presence from disrupting the service. I also asked him to use the presentation of the gospel to penetrate this man's heart. The oppression I felt was lifted, and we worshiped the Lord without interruption. I watched the man as I preached, not out of fear but to see his response to God's truth. He looked around with obvious disdain at all that was happening around him, and he walked out as the final prayer was spoken. I am convinced that he was under the control of a powerful demon.

When I shared that experience with a group of Christians several months later, one man immediately became agitated. He blurted out, "Why didn't you command the demon to come out? Scripture doesn't tell us to pray that a demon won't disrupt the service; it tells us to cast the demon out of the person. That man should have been delivered, but he left in the same bondage he entered under!"

My friend's rebuke first startled me and then bothered me.

Had I failed to do something that God had wanted done? His rebuke also drove me to the Bible, because I wanted to know what God's Word said about the situation. That really is the issue we have to face. It's one thing to read about *Jesus'* works of exorcism, but what about *us* and what about *today*? If demons were actively opposing God's work in the New Testament, shouldn't we expect their opposition today? *Can* we confront demons like Jesus did, and *should* we confront them like Jesus did?

Wrestling with Evil Forces
The spiritual warfare that Jesus exposed during his ministry certainly continues today. The apostle Paul made that point powerfully clear:

> Put on the full armor of God so that you can take your stand against the devil's schemes. For our struggle is not against flesh and blood, but against the rulers, against the authorities, against the powers of this dark world and against the spiritual forces of evil in the heavenly realms. (Ephesians 6:11-12)

Evil angels will attack us and seek to hinder our effectiveness for the Lord. These same demons will seek to oppress and possess people just like they did in the days of the New Testament. As I said in the last chapter, demons may exercise their power in more sophisticated ways in our culture, but their presence is very real.

Chris Kline is host for a Christian radio station in Virginia Beach, Virginia. She has experienced the deceptive power of demons firsthand. As a young woman she pursued a lifestyle centered on drugs, immorality and drunkenness. On May 13, 1974, in the grip of an alcohol- and drug-induced high, Chris heard a voice in her New York City hotel room: "Don't be afraid, Chris. I am God, and I have a message for you." A brilliant white light filled her head and flooded her being with peace. The "voice" now resided in her.

What followed were months of instructions from this inner voice, volumes of automatic writing (more than four thousand pages) and her personal belief that God was trying to get her to produce a book that would convey his message to the world. But the self-destructive, sinful lifestyle continued. Finally, after ten years under Satan's power, Chris trusted Christ as her Savior. Over the following months Chris was set free from the bondage she had known for so long.

Looking back, Chris Kline believes that she had opened herself to demonic oppression by her lifestyle and that she was controlled by a demon pretending to be the inner voice of God. Her testimony is powerful: "Evil spirits tried to destroy me; they came very close to succeeding. Satan came to me as 'an angel of light' but instead of giving me the freedom I wanted, he entangled me slowly but surely in his cords of death."[4]

But Should We Be Casting Out Demons?

I was convinced that the man who came into our church was under demonic influence, but should I have confronted the demon and cast it out as my friend suggested? As I pored over the New Testament, several issues came into clearer focus.

First, we are never directly commanded to cast out demons. Nowhere does the Bible address believers with such a directive. Jesus cast out demons, Jesus authorized the twelve apostles and the seventy-two disciples to have authority over demons, and Philip and Paul commanded demons to leave people. But not once are Christians in general commanded to cast out demons.

What Christians *are* told in Scripture is to *resist* the devil. James gives us this promise: "Submit yourselves, then, to God. Resist the devil, and he will flee from you" (James 4:7). The apostle Peter follows up his description of Satan as a roaring

73

lion seeking someone to devour with a strong command: "Resist him, standing firm in the faith" (1 Peter 5:9). When I have sensed the attacks of Satan in my own life, when he has come to batter me with his accusations or to fill me with fear, I have tried to consciously resist his attack. I have said (at times out loud), "Satan, I resist you and your evil assault on my life. Now according to God's promise you *must* leave me alone."

Another significant conclusion that I gleaned from my study of the Scriptures is that Jesus never sought out people who were demon-possessed; the people always came to Jesus. The demon-oppressed person took the initiative to open the confrontation. I am convinced that I should not have confronted the man who came into our church, because if I had simply walked up to him and commanded the demon to leave him, I would not have been following Jesus' example.

Even my approach of praying for God to restrain any evil influence on our worship service from the man or the evil power in his life has biblical precedent. When Jesus came down from the Mount of Transfiguration, he found nine of his disciples trying to cast a demon out of a young boy, but they were failing. After Jesus rebuked the evil spirit, he said to the disciples, "This kind [of demon] can come out only by prayer" (Mark 9:29). In his exhortation to put on God's armor as protection in the spiritual battle, Paul includes a firm admonition to prayer: "Take the helmet of salvation and the sword of the spirit, which is the word of God. And pray in the Spirit on all occasions with all kinds of prayers and requests. With this in mind, be alert and always keep on praying for all the saints" (Ephesians 6:17-18).

Staying Off the Dead-End Streets

Confidence in the ultimate defeat of Satan and his angels has led some Christians down some unwise (and, at times, unbiblical) paths. I have heard Christians say, "I bind Satan from my family" or "I bind evil spirits from my home." Jude, however, in his little New Testament postcard, warns us about approaching angels, including evil angels, with a casual attitude. Some false teachers had come into the circle of Jude's Christian friends and had begun to speak flippantly about their authority over angelic beings. Jude calls their bluff with this illustration:

Even the archangel Michael, when he was disputing with the devil about the body of Moses, did not dare to bring a slanderous accusation against him, but said, "The Lord rebuke you!" Yet these men speak abusively against whatever they do not understand; . . . these are the very things that destroy them. (Jude 9-10; see also 2 Peter 2:10-11)

As powerful as Michael the archangel is, he did not rebuke Satan in his own authority but appealed to a higher one, the ultimate authority of God himself. When we face demonic power, our confidence comes from the Lord's authority, not our own.

I have also known Christians who see demons behind every situation or difficulty. Our son Kyle went through a time when he had nightmares. In his dreams a cat would jump on his bed or a mouse would run under the closet door. One well-meaning Christian suggested that we cast the demons out of Kyle's bedroom. He even volunteered to come over to our home and pray over the bed and anoint the door to the room. But the Bible doesn't give any spiritual prescriptions like that.

When the congregation at the city of Corinth was pulled apart by dissension, Paul did not tell them to cast out a "spirit of dissension." He told them to "be perfectly united in mind and thought" (1 Corinthians 1:10). The real problem was not demons but the carnal attitude of the Christians. They were spiritual crybabies, and they needed to grow up (1 Corinthians 3:1-4).

When two women in the church at Philippi were at odds with each other, Paul pleaded with them to get along and asked the leader of the congregation to help the women to resolve the issue. There is no instruction to cast out a demon of division or disharmony. In our son's case, a night light and his own prayer that "Kyle would have no bad dreams" brought an end to the nightmares. Neither Jesus nor any other New Testament writer ever attributes anger, lust, broken marriages, murder or greed to demonic powers.

Another disturbing approach to demonic power comes from those who seek to break "demonic strongholds." I heard about one pastor who held a special service on the property where he wanted to build a church building. He was having trouble getting the local zoning commission's approval for his plan, so he tried to "summon the local territorial spirit"—a demon who (according to the pastor) did not want the gospel proclaimed in that area. But no one in the New Testament ever seeks to liberate a city from demonic control before the gospel is preached. Instead, Christians proclaimed the message, and the gospel changed lives!

Although the Bible clearly recognizes the influence of demonic forces in our world that are opposed to God's people, the emphasis of Scripture is on the Christian's personal responsibility to grow in faith and obedience to Christ. Nowhere are we given the right to shift the blame for our sin to demons. "The devil made me do it" is a spiritual cop-out. Our primary focus should be to strive after spiritual maturity and to overcome the drag of the flesh with the help of the Holy Spirit. This approach to the Christian life does not ignore the spiritual warfare that rages against us; it seeks to keep the commands and admonitions of Scripture in proper balance. Several passages suggest that the obedient Christian who is walking in the Spirit has little to fear from demonic influence. Jesus himself prays to the Father for our protection from the evil one (John 17:15; see also 2 Thessalonians 3:3; 1 John 5:18).

The Ministry of Deliverance

If we suspect or know that demonic influence is being exercised over a person we are ministering to, we can and should seek to bring spiritual deliverance into that person's life. But several principles need to be kept in mind.

First, it is crucial to establish the person's relationship with Christ. If the person you are counseling or praying with is a believer, he or she has the Holy Spirit resident within. The Christian can be encouraged to walk in obedience to God and to armor himself against demonic attack. If the person you are dealing with is not a believer, the first step in his or her deliverance is to be born again by faith in Christ. If the individual refuses to believe in Christ, there is little that can be done. Jesus gave a stern warning about casting out a demon and leaving the "house" of a person's heart empty. The original demon will return with seven others more powerful than itself, and the person's final condition will be worse than the first (Matthew 12:43-45).

Second, take the time to explain what your suspicions are. If you simply launch into an exorcism without the person's knowledge or permission, you may frighten or confuse the person into abandoning you as a spiritual friend. I have at times asked a person, "Do you think an evil spirit may be attacking you?" I will follow that question by asking another: "Would you give me your permission to rebuke any evil spirit that may be oppressing or attacking you?"

Some Christian leaders teach that we should try to cast out a demon even if we are not certain of demonic activity, because it can't hurt the person and may help. That idea is dangerous. In the examples of Scripture, no exorcism or deliverance was ever attempted until a direct demonic presence was established. In a highly suggestive or desperate person, a false exorcism may actually produce the symptoms it is designed to relieve.[5]

If the person gives you permission to do so, speak a brief, clear command. The rebuke should always be based on the authority of Christ. "In the name of Jesus Christ, I command any and all evil spirits to leave this person and to remove themselves from his life." Many Christians involved in deliverance ministries tell emotionally charged, dramatic stories of long battles with demons. But there is no indication from the Bible that a long conflict is part of the process. Jesus simply "drove out the spirits with a word" (Matthew 8:16). Jesus also cast out many demons at one time (Mark 5:9-13; Luke 8:30-33). The power over demons comes from the Lord Jesus, not from our own strength.

A third principle to remember is to guard your own heart and mind during the confrontation with demonic forces. Jesus' disciples were unable to cast out a demon from an epileptic boy because at the time they were weak in faith and had not spent enough time in prayer (Matthew 17:20; Mark 9:29). Spiritual warfare is exhausting. Don't open yourself to attack by failing to maintain your own walk of obedience to God. We need to be careful, too, that we don't become overly curious or obsessed with the demonic world. In regard to evil we are to be "infants" (1 Corinthians 14:20) and "innocent" (Romans 16:19). Our focus should be on things that are honorable and pure (Philippians 4:8).

Jesus made it clear to the seventy-two disciples who ministered under his authority that they were not to become proud or rejoice too much about their power over demons. Instead they were to rejoice in their salvation: "Do not rejoice that the spirits submit to you, but rejoice that your names are written in heaven" (Luke 10:20). You can claim another promise of Scripture as you face demonic attack or confrontation: "The God of peace will soon crush Satan under your feet" (Romans 16:20).

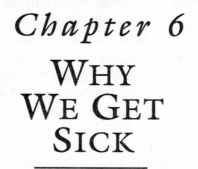

Chapter 6
WHY
WE GET
SICK

*I*f I could have one ability that Jesus had during his earthly ministry, I would choose the ability to heal the sick. I can think of very few things in the human realm more rewarding than restoring the health of a cancer victim or making a child who is stricken with cystic fibrosis whole again. I do not pray with a sick person or visit a hospital room or sit in the home of a dying person without wishing that I had the capacity to bring instant healing to that person's weak and ravaged body.

People in the United States will spend $940 billion on health care this year—almost a trillion dollars trying to get well—and another $100 billion trying to stay well. Every one of us has to face the issue of recovery from sickness, and we have to face it many times in the course of our lives.

The largest category of biblical miracles is miracles of healing.

In the days of Moses, venomous snakes came among the people of Israel as God's judgment for their complaint against his servant. The serpents' bites were painful and deadly. God, in response to Moses' pleading, had him fashion a snake made of bronze, put it on a pole and lift it above the people. Those who were bitten had to do one thing to be healed and live: look at the bronze serpent (Numbers 21:4-9).

The prophet Elisha was told one day that a foreign dignitary—an Aramean military leader named Naaman—was outside his gate. This military leader was afflicted with a disfiguring disease known as leprosy, so he had come to the prophet on the advice of his Israelite servant girl. Naaman was desperate to be healed. But Elisha never even gave him a consultation; he simply told his servant to tell Naaman to go to the Jordan River and dip in it seven times. At first Naaman was outraged at such a ludicrous command, but one of his aides gave him some wise advice. He reminded Naaman that he had come to the prophet of God prepared to pay any price. What would it hurt to simply follow the prophet's suggestion? When Naaman emerged from the Jordan the seventh time, his skin was as clean as the skin of a young child (2 Kings 5:1-14).

Twenty miracles of healing are recorded in the Gospels: the blind were given sight; those with long-term illnesses instantly recovered; children and adults, individuals and groups of people were all healed by a touch or a word from Jesus. In addition to the specific healings recorded in the Gospels, we are told repeatedly in a variety of contexts and settings that great multitudes of people came to Jesus, and he healed them all (Matthew 4:23-24; 8:16-17; Mark 1:32-34; 3:10-12; Luke 6:17-19; 7:21; 13:32).

The early Christians saw miraculous healings too. Just days after the Spirit's coming at Pentecost, Peter and John healed a man who had been crippled from birth. It was a marvelous demonstration of the power of God, and people responded to that miracle just as they should have: "When all the people saw [the healed man] walking and praising God, . . . they were filled with wonder and amazement at what had happened to him" (Acts 3:9-10). The apostle Peter used the interest stirred up by the miracle as an opportunity to proclaim the message of the gospel. He made it clear that the man had been healed by the power of Christ alone (v. 16). The early church fully expected that God would demonstrate his power by stretching out his hand "to *heal* and perform miraculous signs and wonders through the name of [his] holy servant Jesus" (Acts 4:30).

With so many miracles of healing recorded in Scripture, we naturally want to know if the same miraculous works are available to us today. Healing is a hot issue among Christians. While all believers would agree that the Lord alone is the one who heals us (Exodus 15:26), different groups of Christians give different answers to the question of how God heals, or even *if* God heals miraculously today. My goal in these chapters on healing is not to pit one group of Christians against another. Instead, I want to examine what the Scriptures say and reach some conclusions based not on opinion or on a particular tradition but on biblical truth. I won't satisfy everyone, nor will I answer every question about healing. I do think, however, that we Christians can come to broad areas of agreement and biblical unity in our understanding of physical healing.

One approach that has helped me get a clearer perspective on healing has been to look at the reasons we get sick in the first place. David Thompson, a friend of mine who pastors a church in Pocatello, Idaho, has gleaned seven reasons from the Bible that explain why we get sick.

The Body Is Weak

First, we get sick because our human bodies are weak and

limited. We may feel strong at times and in certain circumstances show amazing resilience. But one microscopic bacterium or virus can put the strongest of us down in bed—or in the hospital. Human cells in just about any organ or region of the body can begin to grow without restraint and become a cancerous rampage. We get run down. We become exhausted because of our stress-filled lives. We really are fragile beings.

When the apostle Paul was in prison, the Philippian congregation sent Epaphroditus to Paul to help meet his needs. Epaphroditus worked to the point of exhaustion. He became ill and almost died. God in his mercy brought Epaphroditus back to health, but Paul called on the church to honor this man because he "almost died for the work of Christ, risking his life to make up for the help you could not give me" (Philippians 2:25-30).

Sometimes Christians get sick—even Christians who are serving Christ and who are doing the work of Christ. Our bodies are vulnerable to disease and exhaustion and weakness. We may honor and care for our bodies well, but we may still become sick at times.

A Fallen World

Another reason we get sick is that we live in an imperfect environment. A few years ago between pastorates I worked for an environmental testing laboratory. One day I picked up several dozen jars of oil that was contaminated with a witch's brew of chemicals, including PCB and a host of cancer-causing organic compounds. I remember thinking as I drove my little Plymouth Horizon toward the laboratory, *If I get in an accident, I am a goner!* But the fact is we live surrounded by hazardous substances. Doctors and nurses and dentists have to take elaborate precautions against HIV, the virus that causes AIDS. Even our food may introduce viruses or pesticides or herbicides into our bodies that will make us sick. Young pastor Timothy apparently had a problem with the water in Ephesus, so the apostle Paul prescribed a little wine for easing his "stomach ailments and . . . frequent illnesses" (1 Timothy 5:23). Sometimes elements in our environment make us sick.

We live in a world that is not only polluted physically; it is also polluted spiritually. The sin of our parents, Adam and Eve, brought a curse on the physical world that we inhabit. All of creation is in "bondage to decay" (Romans 8:21). We are surrounded by constant reminders that we live in a fallen world: drunken drivers cause horrible accidents, gang members shoot and injure young people, even parents may abuse and violate their own children.

Physical disabilities and birth defects and congenital diseases are reminders of the same sad truth. Many of Jesus' healings were directed toward people who had these kinds of disabilities. He healed those who were lame and blind and epileptic. Friends of ours have a son afflicted with a rare growth disorder. He has had a long series of painful operations and procedures to try to correct the problem. Other friends had a beautiful baby, but within months signs of Down syndrome began to appear. Why? Why does God allow such circumstances in the lives of people who love Christ and want to serve him?

An eighty-year-old woman in our congregation was attacked and raped in her own home. When I went to the hospital, I took her bruised face gently in my hands and choked out through my tears, "I am so sorry this happened to you." She replied with such calm: "Pastor, we live in a sinful world."

I don't have many answers for those who have physical disabilities or who give birth to babies with Down syndrome—except that God does not make mistakes. When Moses complained to the Lord that he was not eloquent enough to speak before Pharaoh, God said, "Who gave man his mouth? Who makes him deaf or mute? Who gives him sight or makes him blind? Is it not I, the LORD?" (Exodus 4:11). Forty years later Moses had accepted that hard truth. In his song of praise to God he shouts, "I will proclaim the name of the LORD. Oh, praise the greatness of our God! He is the Rock, his works are perfect, and all his ways are just. A faithful God who does no wrong, upright and just is he" (Deuteronomy 32:3-4).

Once to Die
The third biblical reason we get sick may sound a little heartless, but we have to face it eventually. We may get sick even as Christians because it is appointed by God that we will eventually die, and one of the ways we die is through sickness. Because of Adam's disobedience to God, sin entered the world of humanity, and riding on sin's coattails was death (Romans 5:12). God told Adam and Eve that if they disobeyed his word to them, they would die—and they did. From the day of their sin forward, physical deterioration set in. They plodded inevitably toward death. Men and women, according to Hebrews 9:27, are "destined to die." Job lamented that the days of human life are "swifter than a weaver's shuttle" and then come to an end (Job 7:6). Our lives on earth are like a cloud that evaporates or a spark that flies up from a fire only to quickly cool and die.

Nowhere in Scripture are followers of Christ guaranteed lives free from sickness or suffering or pain or sorrow. People who shout claims like that from the television or radio are not telling you the truth. Jesus said that following him would be like carrying a cross. I am not saying that the Christian life is drudgery. We have sources of joy and comfort and peace that the average worldling knows nothing about. But as long as we are in these bodies of flesh we will see deterioration and decay and ultimately death. The final release from sickness and pain will not come through a miraculous healing but through a miraculous resurrection of our bodies to life forever.

Put to the Test

Job is an example of another reason a Christian may get sick. Job got sick because Satan was trying to turn Job's heart away from trust in the Lord. From Satan's perspective, Job's ordeal was a temptation to abandon faith in God; from God's perspective, he allowed Job to be stricken as a test and proof of his faith. Satan wanted Job to *fail* the test; God provided all Job needed to *pass* the test.

I have always been fascinated by how Job's trial developed. It started in heaven, not on earth—and God challenged Satan! God said to Satan, "Have you considered my servant Job? He is blameless and upright and fears God." Satan replied, "Of course! Who wouldn't serve you if he were protected like Job! I can't get near him." So God gave all that Job had into Satan's hand, and that cruel enemy pummeled Job to the limit of his permission. Satan took everything, including the lives of Job's children. But still Job maintained a confident trust in God.

When Satan was confronted again, God said, "You were wrong, Satan. Job still loves me." Satan said, "Of course! Who wouldn't love you if he were protected like Job! You won't let me put him to the real test!" So God allowed Satan to strike Job to the deepest part of his being, short of taking his life. This time Satan did not test Job with depression or divorce or financial reversal. Satan's most penetrating bullet was sickness. Job's ordeal began with a severe skin disease that covered his entire body with draining and intensely painful boils. He also suffered from fever, drastic weight loss, fits of weeping, sleeplessness, nightmares, putrid breath, failing vision, rotting teeth and a haggard look! Job was in absolute anguish—in far more pain than most of us ever will face. But in spite of all that Satan threw at him, Job maintained his trust in God. He struggled like we all do, but he endured the test by God's grace.

My phone rang not long ago, and I answered to hear sobs on the other end. A man in our church family is in the advanced stages of bone cancer. His tearful wife wanted me to pray because he was having a lot of pain. You also may be suffering deeply as you read this book. Sometimes God may allow sickness to come into our lives to test our faith—and to silence our enemy.

Sufficient Grace

Job's endurance leads to the fifth reason we may get sick as believers. God may allow sickness or physical affliction to strike us so that we will learn to rely as never before on God's grace and faithful love. God has not abandoned us in our sickness; we are not alone in a hospital room or on the operating table or in the dark hours of pain.

Even though the apostle Paul suffered from a serious physical problem and pleaded with the Lord on three separate occasions to remove the affliction, each time God responded the same way: "My grace is sufficient for you, for my power is made perfect in weakness" (2 Corinthians 12:9). Well-meaning Christians drop this verse like a Bible bullet on people who are suffering, thinking it will magically make things better. But if we could come to this passage with new eyes and a receptive heart, we would find a powerful encouragement in times of pain or despair.

During a time of great emotional pain in my own life, I felt like God was far away from me—not angry with me or uncaring, just distant. When I shared that feeling with a friend of mine, he gave me a wise perspective that I've never forgotten: "Sometimes God makes us feel like he is far from us even when he is very near. He makes us feel that way so we will search for him more diligently and long for his fellowship more deeply." In the psalmist's words, "I sought the LORD, and he answered me" (Psalm 34:4). Sometimes God allows us to get sick so that we will trust him more.

For God's Glory
Jesus and his disciples came upon a beggar one day who had been blind from birth. Maybe the man wore a sign announcing his condition in hope that people would be prompted to drop more coins into his cup. The disciples saw the man as a theological problem: "Who sinned," they asked, "this man or his parents, that he was born blind?" (John 9:2). The disciples had been taught that a disability was punishment from God for a specific sin—either the parents' sin or the baby's. The rabbis believed that a baby's kicking in the womb was evidence that the baby was committing prebirth sinful acts.

Jesus said that the man's blindness was not the direct result of anyone's personal sin. Instead, "this happened so that the work of God might be displayed in his life" (v. 3). Later, Jesus was trying to explain his reason for not returning immediately to the town of Bethany even though his friend Lazarus was sick. He explained that the ultimate end of Lazarus's sickness would not be death but "for God's glory so that God's Son may be glorified through it" (John 11:4).

A sixth biblical answer to why we get sick is because God may desire to raise us up from that sickness in order to demonstrate his power and display his glory. When another believer is sick and we pray for his recovery and God responds by raising him up, we are prompted to give God praise and honor. We stand in awe of God's power, and our own hearts are encouraged. All that worshipful response pleases God.

My brother-in-law Dick Reynolds became ill one evening at work in a General Motors plant. The next day he had brain surgery to remove an abnormal cluster of blood vessels that had begun to leak blood into his brain. Several serious complications followed. Dick was in the hospital for months and many times was near death. But the church prayed fervently—and in time God raised him up. Not every physical effect of his surgery has been removed, but whenever Dick prays or cracks a joke, it's a reminder to all of us of God's great power, and we are prompted to thank God again for what he has done in Dick's life.

Confess Your Sins So That You May Be Healed

The final reason we may become sick is easily misunderstood and misused. The Bible clearly says that Christians may become sick as a chastening from God for sin in their lives. Not *all* sickness is chastening for sin, but sickness *can* be the evidence of God's reproof. The great king Uzziah followed the Lord obediently until he desired the place in God's program reserved only for Israel's priests. When Uzziah entered the holy place, God struck him with leprosy (2 Chronicles 26:19-20). Even though I believe that Uzziah repented of his arrogance, the leprosy was never removed.

In the church at Corinth, the Christians were using the occasion of the Lord's Supper as an excuse for drunkenness and petty displays of divisiveness. The apostle Paul issued a stern rebuke to the church and added that because of their carnal attitude "many among you are weak and sick, and a number have fallen asleep [that is, have died]" (1 Corinthians 11:30). Ananias and Sapphira were killed by the Lord for lying to the church and to the Holy Spirit (Acts 5:1-11). James, in the context of his discussion on anointing those who are sick and praying for their recovery, adds, "If [the sick person] has sinned, he will be forgiven. Therefore confess your sins to each other and pray for each other so that you may be healed" (James 5:15-16). If sickness comes upon us as God's chastening, we will not recover unless we confess the sin and walk in obedience to God once again.

Maybe you sense that you are under God's chastening in your life right now. I need to remind you that God disciplines his children out of love (Hebrews 12:6). If you had a harsh earthly father, you may struggle with that truth. But God's discipline is not designed to drive you away from him; it is designed to draw you back to him. When chastening comes, respond by confessing the sin fully to God. You will discover that when you turn in repentance toward God, the Father runs to welcome you back into his fellowship.

New Perspective

The child of God has the privilege of seeing all of life through the lens of God's goodness. Not every experience we go through is pleasant or fair; sometimes life can seem very cruel. But standing in the shadows is a loving Father who allows nothing to overtake us that we cannot bear.

Understanding *why* we get sick helps us understand how God may work to make us well—or why God may not heal us in this life. I have been in too many hospital rooms to ever think that God abandons us when we are sick. When we are flat on our backs, the only place we can look is up!

Chapter 7

WHAT TO DO WHEN YOU GET SICK

*T*he man stood up from the back pew and began to make his way to the front of the church. As people saw him walking forward, many began to weep. He slowly knelt at the altar in obvious pain. Within minutes more than a dozen people had surrounded him. Some of the people were gently touching him; all were praying, all were crying. The man who came forward had cancer. We had watched his decline for several months. On this night he and his church were praying for healing.

What should we do when serious sickness comes into our lives? I have gleaned five steps from the biblical record that every Christian should take when he or she becomes sick. Taking these steps will not guarantee healing from God; not taking the steps will not limit God's ability to work powerfully in our lives. They are steps of obedience and steps of faith that acknowledge both God's sovereign power over us as his children and God's ability to work miraculously to meet our needs.

Pray for God's Healing

When I graduated from seminary, I held a view of miracles that theologians call the cessationist position. I believed that *all* miracles and supernatural healings ceased with the death of the apostles. For many years as a pastor I prayed for those who were sick but never specifically asked God to miraculously heal anyone.

It wasn't until a godly elder in my congregation pointed me to a verse in James that I realized how wrong I had been. Though I had read the verse dozens of times, I had never really applied the truth consistently to my life: "You do not have, because you do not ask God" (James 4:2)—and the elder was right! In my years of ministry I had never seen a person recover from sickness in anything close to miraculous fashion. I had seen lots of sick people get better over time, but never anything even approaching the healings of Jesus. So I began to pray differently.

Today when I visit someone who is sick or who is facing surgery or who has been diagnosed with an incurable disease, I ask God in prayer to heal that person. I don't demand healing; I ask for it. My prayer isn't the arrogant command of a television showman; it is the humble cry of a child of God.

I also acknowledge when I pray that God is far greater and wiser than I am. I ask for his healing, but I also submit to his will. I've been challenged a few times about praying like that. One man told me that when I pray "if it be your will," I am demonstrating a lack of faith. He, of course, believed that it was *always* God's will to heal. As I looked at Scripture, however, I disagreed with his conclusion. Sometimes when God allowed faithful believers to become sick, it was clearly his will. When we ask God to do something "if it is his will," we are simply confessing that we don't know with certainty what his will is in this particular situation.

To think that merely expressing *our* will as Christians makes something *God's* will is wrong. Prayer is not our manipulation of God. Prayer is a conforming of our will to his will. Sometimes when we ask God to heal "if it is his will," he will grant that request. I have seen it happen. Sometimes God will begin to change our hearts so that we ask for something else—our request is conformed to his will. Sometimes God will not grant our request but leads us instead to rest in his wisdom and care.

That is why it is important in our prayers not only to talk to God but also to listen to him. Waiting on the Lord is a lost spiritual discipline for most of us. We burst into God's presence, blurt out our requests and then move on to other things. But when we learn to wait silently and openly before him, we will find the Lord working powerfully in our lives. He may begin to change what we desire or give us greater insight into his will. The Spirit of God within us might give us a sense of assurance of what God's will is or increase our confidence in God's love and concern for us. When we pray for God's healing, we must be sure to listen for God's still, quiet response.

In certain situations I have found myself coming to God over and over with a request to be healed or to heal someone else. Paul asked the Lord on three separate occasions that his physical affliction, his thorn in the flesh, be removed (2 Corinthians 12:8). Jesus in the garden of Gethsemane asked the Father if it were possible to remove the cup of suffering that stretched out before him. Then, after he found the disciples sleeping, Jesus prayed again, saying the same words (Mark 14:36-39). One popular misconception among Christians is that if we pray about a need more than once, we are guilty of the "vain repetition" Jesus warned about in Matthew

6:7 (KJV). But following the example of Jesus and Paul, earnest, humble prayer offered many times for the same need merely demonstrates how deeply we sense the burden of that need in our lives.

Jesus admonished, "Keep on asking and it will be given to you; keep on seeking and you will find; keep on knocking and the door will be opened to you" (Matthew 7:7, my translation). If God wants us to stop praying about a specific situation, he will make that clear. Until we have the assurance of God's will, however, we should keep on praying. We may fast in order to focus our praying or gather with others for corporate prayer or, even as Jesus did, spend an entire night in prayer. But the Spirit of God's encouragement to our hearts to "devote [ourselves] to prayer, being watchful and thankful" (Colossians 4:2) should spur us to persevere in our praying, confident that our Father delights to hear his child crying out in humble dependence on him.

If you or a family member or another believer in your church is sick, pray. Ask God to heal his child. Ask in faith. Ask in submission to a sovereign, loving Father.

Seek Medical Help
After you have prayed, get off your knees and call the doctor! Seeking medical help is not an evidence of a lack of faith. Medical care may be one of the means that God uses to answer your prayer for healing. God has created substances that can be made into medicine to treat diseases and to encourage healing. All of God's created world is "very good" (Genesis 1:31) and should be received and used with thankfulness (Psalm 24:1).

Wayne Grudem suggests that when medicine is available and we refuse it, we are "forcing a test" on the Lord. We are insisting that God perform a miracle of healing instead of healing us through medicine or a doctor's care.[1] Our confidence, of course, is not in the doctors or in medicines; our confidence for healing is in God. But we need to realize that God has made our bodies to respond to proper care and has given humanity wisdom in how to treat certain diseases. God may choose to work miraculously to bring healing to our bodies. He may also choose to work through the natural laws that he has established to bring recovery and health. Normal recovery over a period of time is no less a work of God than miraculous, instantaneous healing. Recovery over time in response to the prayers of God's people can be just as awe-inspiring a testimony of God's power as an instantaneous miracle of healing.

Two biblical examples press home the point of seeking medical help after asking the Lord for healing. In the thirty-ninth year of his reign as king of Judah, Asa was afflicted with a disease in his feet. The disease apparently came as the last loving attempt of the Lord to turn Asa from his path of oppression and unbelief. The disease was severe. But "even in his illness [Asa] did not seek help from the Lord, but only from the physicians" (2 Chronicles 16:12). Two years later Asa died. Asa put his trust in doctors when he should have sought the Lord. No doctor or prescription drug can cure what God intends to use as chastening. At the same time, no disease or physical condition can resist God's power when he purposes to heal.

Two hundred years after Asa's death, another king got sick. Hezekiah was at the point of death. The prophet Isaiah told him that he should put his house in order because he was going to die. The king responded by praying fervently to the Lord to spare his life. The sickness accomplished what God desired in Hezekiah's life—it turned him back to wholehearted obedience to the Lord. When God saw the desired response in Hezekiah, God gave a new message to Isaiah: "Go back and tell Hezekiah,

'. . . I have heard your prayer and seen your tears; I will heal you. On the third day from now you will go up to the temple of the LORD. I will add fifteen years to your life' " (2 Kings 20:4-6).

When you become sick, pray. It is the Lord who heals you. Then seek competent medical care. The apostle Paul (perhaps after consultation with his personal physician, Luke) prescribed a little wine for young Timothy's stomach ailments (1 Timothy 5:23). God has allowed human beings to gain incredible insight into how the human body functions. God is the one who has permitted us to discover drugs and technology to help the body overcome sickness. Those good gifts are for our benefit and help. Constantly keep in mind, however, that God can heal even when medical means fail. A woman who had spent all her living on doctors and who could not be cured by any of them simply touched Jesus' garment one day and was instantly healed (Luke 8:43-44).

My father often tells the story of his experience in Bible college in the early 1940s. Other students would stand up in chapel and tell how they had prayed for money and the next day a check came in the mail from someone they did not even know. My dad said, however, that when he prayed for money, God always gave him a job to earn it. The prayer was still answered, just not in a spectacular way.

I have prayed many times for God's healing for myself and for others. Occasionally God will answer in an immediate, miraculous healing. Most of the time, however, the healing comes through rest, good diet and qualified medical care. Going to a doctor is not lack of faith; it is an act of wisdom.

In the early 1970s a brilliant Old Testament scholar left his teaching position in an evangelical seminary to start a new church. His following in northern Indiana grew rapidly and created quite a stir, even in the secular media. Hobart Freeman preached a gospel of healing. His followers were told that they were not to go to a doctor or a hospital ever again. Even dentists and optometrists were unnecessary. The unsaved world might need such spiritual crutches, but true believers had access to continuous miraculous healing. Pregnant women were told that one of the group's midwives would assist them in the birth of their children.

Freeman's message sounded utopian—until a baby died in childbirth from relatively minor complications that the midwife was not trained to handle. Then another child died. The zealous preacher announced that the children had died because their parents had not fully believed the message of healing. In time, the huge auditorium his followers had built began to empty. Hobart Freeman died a few years later from untreated disease in his own body.

Those who proclaim a health-and-wealth gospel have a warped and unbiblical perspective on healing. Be very careful that what you hear from the television preacher or crusade healer squares with the teaching of God's Word. Embracing a partial, distorted belief about healing can be dangerous to your health.

Confess Any Known Sin in Your Life

Not all sickness is the result of personal sin—but (as we have already seen) sometimes sickness may come upon a believer as God's chastening. The Lord does not reprimand us in anger or out of hatred; he disciplines those he loves. God loves us too much to let us continue on in disobedience or indifference.

When you become sick, take time to honestly and carefully examine yourself. Are you walking in disobedience in some area? Have you started down a path of compromise or sin? Have you resisted God's conviction or direction about some relationship or personal activity?

I need to caution you about getting *too* introspective. I have had people say to me, "Two years ago I did something, but I confessed it and dealt with it—but maybe I'm being punished now for what I did then." Discipline is not punishment. The penalty of our sins was fully paid by Christ through his death on the cross. God's reproof comes into our lives when we refuse to confess and turn away from sin. We harden our hearts against God to the point that only drastic action on his part will get our attention.

In my experience, when a Christian is under God's discipline, that person knows it. When they examine their life, they know immediately why God has allowed a particular sickness to come. The question is, will they repent? If you are sick and you know that God has allowed that sickness to come because of disobedience, confess that sin fully to God. Admit that it is what God says it is—sin. Then change your mind and attitude and life. With God's help, abandon that sin. Enlist other trusted believers to hold you accountable. Only then will healing come.

Several years ago I developed a string of severe respiratory infections. I knew why they were coming. I had confessed an area of sin in my life to God, but I had not dealt honestly with the other people whom the sin had affected. God's Spirit had pressed on me at times to openly confess, but I had resisted— and I got sick. My physician was a sensitive Christian. When I came into his office for the third infection in three months and his best antibiotics seemed to have little effect, he said, "Doug, this is more than just a physical problem. More is going on here. I'm available to talk anytime." As I left his office, tears began to stream down my face. I had been found out! That doctor's loving intervention began the long, difficult process of repentance in my life.

Our God will not be mocked. What we sow is exactly what we reap. In his grace, God does not throw us aside when we walk away from him. He follows us—and loves us—and puts every obstacle he can in our path to get us to turn back to him. When we come to our senses and resolve to return to the Father, as we swing around to head back, we find him right there ready to embrace us. The hard consequences of our disobedience may still have to be faced, but we do not face them alone. Down the painful path of confession and repentance and restoration, our Father walks with us.

Ask to Be Anointed

Healing can come after any one of the steps I have outlined. You may earnestly ask God to heal you and find yourself better. You may pray and then go to the doctor, and as you take care of your body's needs, you will get better. Confession alone may bring healing if the sickness in your life is God's discipline.

But if the sickness persists, a fourth biblical step is appropriate. James, in his little New Testament letter, tells those who are sick to ask the spiritual leaders of the church to anoint them with oil. The practice of anointing the sick with oil is one of the most neglected biblical practices, to our great loss as Christians. I often ask pastors I meet in various contexts if they anoint those who are sick as part of their pastoral ministry. Most of the time the response I get is not opposition to the idea but ignorance. These pastors do not have any objections to it; they just don't do it.

Within the Roman Catholic Church anointing of the sick is considered one of the sacraments. Once referred to as extreme unction, it was primarily the final preparation of a person for death. In recent years the "idea behind this anointing is to offer the healing grace of God to the infirm and the aged."[2] A few Protestant Christians have taken a wholesale approach to anointing and anoint anyone for any kind of need.

Several years ago I determined to study the passage in James and simply obey what it said. I began to teach the passage to my congregation, and in time we began to do what God instructed us to do. The passage is fairly straightforward:

Is any one of you sick? He should call the elders of the church to pray over him and anoint him with oil in the name of the Lord. And the prayer offered in faith will make the sick person well; the Lord will raise him up. If he has sinned, he will be forgiven. Therefore confess your sins to each other and pray for each other so that you may be healed. The prayer of a righteous man is powerful and effective. (James 5:14-16)

Remember as you think about this passage that James wrote one of the first New Testament books. This instruction was given to the early church, when miraculous works were still widely displayed and when gifts of healing were prominent in the church. But James writes to a church overseen by elders, not apostles, and he gives them and us a pattern for handling sickness in the church family. James places three requirements on the sick person.

First, he or she has to be sick. The Greek word James uses means, literally, "without strength"; it was a word often used to refer to physical sickness. The point we need to grasp from James's choice of words is that the practice of anointing is for those who are seriously sick, for those who seem to be without strength in themselves for recovery. I do not think anointing is appropriate for minor ailments, nor is it appropriate if the person has not worked through the other steps. If someone who has not prayed personally for healing or has not gone to a doctor for medical care asks me for an anointing, I encourage him or her to take those steps first.

The second requirement placed on the sick person is that he or she must be a Christian, a believer in Jesus Christ. "Is any one *of you* [literally, among you] sick?" Anointing is a family matter. It is not for the unbeliever or the general public.

The seriously sick believer is then to take the initiative in asking for the anointing. He or she is to call the elders of the church for prayer and anointing with oil. I have no biblical authority to simply show up at a sick person's home for an anointing. The sick person is to call. I think this means, too, that I am not to have an anointing for someone who is unconscious or for an infant. The sick person has a vital part to play in what goes on during an anointing, so he or she must be capable of understanding and participating in the process.

Once the sick person has asked for an anointing, the elders of the church are responsible to answer that call. If you are part of a church tradition that does not have specifically designated "elders," they are, in generic terms, those who are responsible for the spiritual leadership of the church. Certainly a pastor is an elder, and other mature, spiritual leaders can also fill this role. James implies that more than one elder will participate. God may work through any elder's prayer to bring healing. The elders are responsible to pray over the sick person and to anoint the person with oil. I usually have the elders put gentle hands on the sick person as I put olive oil on my fingers and apply the oil to the person's forehead. A pastor friend of mine believes that just as all the elders are to pray, all the elders should anoint. Each elder in his church applies oil to the sick person's head as he prays for God's healing.

Even though oil was used as a medicine in the ancient world, I do not think James is simply suggesting the use of medicine. (One commentator on James suggests that the elders give the person a good rub-down to stimulate blood flow and healing!) Oil is frequently used in Scripture to picture the work of the Holy Spirit. Kings and priests were anointed with oil as a symbol of their empowerment for ministry (Exodus 30:30; 1 Samuel 10:1, 10; 16:13). The oil used in the anointing is a visible reminder of our absolute dependence on the Holy Spirit for healing (2 Corinthians 1:21-22; 1 John 2:20). There is no power in the sick person; there is no power in the oil or the elders; all the power is in God.

The elders are to anoint the sick person "in the name of the Lord," that is, at the Lord's command and with the Lord's authority. Everything in an anointing should focus on the Lord. The spiritual leaders need to make very clear that there is no magic in this process. The results are not based on which elder anoints or which elders pray or on saying special words or going through a particular ritual procedure. To the world that rejects Christ, anointing seems foolish and insignificant, but God often uses weak and foolish things to demonstrate his power and to confound human wisdom.

When the sick person has fulfilled the biblical requirements and when the elders have carried out their spiritual responsibilities, the results are placed in the hands of God. That truth is vital to a proper understanding of these verses. The results are in the hands of a sovereign God who has the power to give them and the power to withhold them.

The first result is the one most often misunderstood. James says, "The prayer offered in faith will make the sick person well." The NIV translation makes it sound like the healing is dependent on the faith of the elders: if they pray in faith, the person will get well; if the person does not recover, the elders did not pray with faith—or with enough faith.

I do not think that is what James meant in this passage, however. To argue that healing depends solely on our faith or on the elders' faith would also suggest that if our faith were great enough, we would never die. What James actually *says* is this: "The prayer of faith will restore the sick." I am persuaded that the prayer of faith is a particular prayer given by God through the elders when he intends to bring healing. If the prayer of faith is energized in an elder or collectively in the elders, the sick one *will* recover. "The Lord," James continues, "*will* raise him up." The prayer of faith is, after all, a prayer, and like all prayer it stresses our willingness to rest on the wisdom and provision of God. When the prayer of faith is given by God, it accomplishes his purpose and the sick one gets better. The healing may be immediate or it may be gradual, but the Lord works powerfully to do what doctors or medicine or the elders or the sick one could never do.

Whenever I teach on healing and anointing the sick, someone always asks, "Do the elders know if the prayer of faith has been given?" My answer has two parts. Over time, everyone will know if the prayer of faith was given because the sick person will either recover or continue to deteriorate. At the time of the anointing, I usually cannot tell if the prayer of faith has been energized in us, but occasionally I can.

A few years ago, a woman in our congregation with a long history of heart disease had to go into the hospital for some intensive tests. Further heart surgery did not seem to be an option. She asked to be anointed, and after the anointing I almost said, "Clara, you will be fine. I'm sure of it." But I kept it to myself. The next day the doctors found nothing wrong. They were amazed that her heart was in such good shape. The Lord had done a remarkable work of power in response to her obedience and prayer.

On the other side of the coin, I participated in an anointing for a wonderful Christian woman who had brain cancer, and as we left her home, I knew in my heart that she would not recover. Those insights from the Lord have not come very often, but when they have I have been overwhelmed by the intensity with which they came into my mind and heart.

James adds one more statement to his explanation of anointing: "If [the sick person] has sinned, he will be forgiven. Therefore confess your sins to each other and pray for each other so that you may be healed" (James 5:15-16). I conclude from James's words that it is particularly important in the context of an anointing service to stress to the sick person that he or she should make full confession to God of any known sin. An open, clean heart before the Lord is the vital element the sick person must bring to the anointing. I also urge the elders who are participating to prayerfully examine their hearts as well so that there is nothing in us that will grieve the Spirit or hinder his working. This aspect of confession is why I do not open an anointing service to anyone who wants to attend. I think it is important that those who participate recognize that their spiritual condition before the Lord has a dramatic impact on what takes place during and after the anointing.

If you are seriously sick, prayerfully consider asking the spiritual leaders in your local church to anoint you and pray for your healing. Anointing is not a guarantee of healing; it is not a magic act. It is a practice that God has given his church and that God may choose to honor and bless as we humbly obey him.

Rest Fully in God's Care
Each of the steps I have described is designed to make us realize our total dependence on the Lord for every aspect of our lives, including our physical health. As you pray and seek good medical care and even ask to be anointed, God may raise you up from your sickness. If he does, give him praise and honor. But God, in the same wisdom and love, may *not* choose to heal you. Don't think that God has stopped loving you or that he loves you less than other believers. It is the depth of his love that he wants to demonstrate to you even in sickness or disability.

Obey what God has said to you in his Word and then submit to his will. You may think that sounds like giving up—or giving in—and it is! But we are not giving in to fate or chance or despair but to the care and concern of a loving Father. Your prayer for healing may be answered when God heals you permanently by taking you into the presence of Christ forever.

The songs that delight the heart of God are not so much those sung in the good times of health and prosperity but those sung through tears in the darkest hours of trial and pain.

My flesh and my heart may fail,
   but God is the strength of my heart
   and my portion forever. . . .
But as for me, it is good to be near God.
   I have made the Sovereign LORD my refuge.
   (Psalm 73:26, 28)

Chapter 8

"DO YOU HAVE ENOUGH FAITH?"

I *was already running late for our midweek service as I hurried* down the hospital corridor. The woman sitting in a wheelchair watched me intently as I approached. I gave her a weak smile and kept walking.

"Hey!" she shouted after me. "Are you a preacher?"

My first thought was *Is it that obvious?* My next thought was *I'll keep moving and pretend I didn't hear her.* The next thought was a gentle nudge from the Spirit of God. I stopped, turned around, walked back to her and said, "Yes, I am. Why do you ask?"

Her response broke my heart. "Why doesn't God heal me? I've prayed and prayed, but I don't get better. My pastor told me that if I had enough faith, God would answer my prayer. What more can I do?" And she began to sob.

When I walked into the church building that evening, I was *really* late. The congregation had started the prayer service without me, but I was able to share the reason for my late arrival at the end of the service. I told them about this dear woman and how I had taken the time to explain to her that God had not left her alone and that her Father was not sitting in heaven dangling the gift of healing over her head while she tried to whip up more faith in him.

I have met many more people like that woman since that encounter in the hospital. Many Christians suffer in sorrow or are drowning in despair because they have been told or have come to believe something about God's miraculous power that just does not square with biblical truth. A trusted television preacher or pious friend or a bestselling book has proclaimed to them a particular path to complete physical healing or financial recovery or the restoration of a marriage. But as hard as these saints have tried, they have never seemed to receive the gift that was promised.

As I examine some of the popular claims associated with miracles and healing in the light of the Scriptures, I will direct my comments toward the claims that are made, not toward the teachers who promote them. Most of the claims are based in part on a biblical promise, but a promise so twisted that the end result is completely unbiblical. I hope that what I say will help all of us approach the issue of miracles from a balanced, biblical viewpoint. I hope too that I will encourage some Christians who may be suffering spiritually and emotionally because they are waiting for a miracle based on unbiblical hope.

Myth No. 1: "If You Just Had More Faith . . ."

Probably the most repeated claim about healing or miraculous intervention is represented by the woman in the hospital. Those who promote a health-and-wealth gospel tell us that we can expect to be made rich and healthy according to our faith. Many of those who promote themselves as "faith healers" use the same claim to their distinct advantage. If a person who comes to their healing crusade is actually healed, the "healer" points to it as a demonstration of the power of God; if the sick person is *not* healed, the "healer" says that it is the sick person's fault: if the person just had more faith, he or she would be healed. Without faith, they say, it is impossible tó please God (true so far). Even Jesus could not heal some people in Nazareth because of their lack of faith (still a true statement). Therefore, if the sick person had more faith, or the right kind of faith, or would just speak the "word of faith," he or she would be healed. The sick person who goes away unhealed leaves under an enormous burden of guilt.

If you look at the miracles that Jesus performed, faith often played a crucial role in healing. Jesus healed a woman who believed that just touching one of Jesus' garments would bring relief from years of personal pain and embarrassment. Jesus responded to her trust by saying, "Daughter, your faith has healed you. Go in peace" (Luke 8:43-48). In the same flow of events Jesus said to Jairus, a grieving father whose daughter was dying, "Don't be afraid; just believe, and she will be healed" (v. 50). Earlier in Luke's story, Jesus healed a paralytic in response to the faith of the men who brought the sick man to Jesus (Luke 5:20—"When Jesus saw *their* faith").

Faith is a crucial element in every aspect of the Christian life, including healing. Without faith, it is impossible to please God (Hebrews 11:6). James warns us that when we ask anything of God, we "must believe and not doubt" (James 1:6). The person who is "double-minded," the person who prays without faith, "should not think he will receive anything from the Lord" (v. 7). However, our faith is not in the *prayer* but in the *person* to whom we pray. We are not called to believe that prayer alone

107

will produce the answer we want (or the answer we *think* we want); we are called to believe that God hears our prayers and responds to his children as a loving, wise Father (Luke 11:11-13).

Furthermore, in the same context as the miracles connected to faith, Luke records several miracles in which the person's faith did not have a direct connection to the healing. Jesus raised the dead son of the widow living in Nain, and the context makes it obvious that no one in the funeral crowd even knew who Jesus was or what he was able to do in the situation (Luke 7:11-16). Jesus cured the demon-possessed man in the region of the Gerasenes with no indication given of the man's faith until after Jesus had miraculously set him free (Luke 8:26-39). A crippled woman was healed of her infirmity, and no mention is made of faith (Luke 13:10-17). In John's Gospel, Jesus healed a man who had been an invalid for thirty-eight years and who had no idea who Jesus was (John 5:1-13).

There was one occasion when Jesus was hindered from doing miracles. He had come to his hometown of Nazareth and had been met with cynical unbelief toward his teaching and wisdom. Matthew explains that Jesus "did not do many miracles there because of their lack of faith" (Matthew 13:58). Mark's account is more direct: "[Jesus] could not do any miracles there. . . . And he was amazed at their lack of faith" (Mark 6:5-6). This incident in Nazareth does *not*, however, justify the claim that a person does not receive a miracle because he or she does not have enough faith. The people of Nazareth refused to believe in Jesus at all. They mocked his claim to be God's Anointed One.

People seeking healing from God today, like the woman I encountered in the hospital, have faith in Christ. They are already believers. The excuse that many modern healers give for their failure to heal is not that the person does not have faith but that the sick person does not have *enough* faith. Nowhere does the Bible validate that reason for a lack of healing. God may choose not to heal a believer, but it is not connected to a lack of faith.

Myth No. 2: "Healing Is Provided in the Atonement"
Another claim that has gained a wide audience is that Jesus died on the cross not only for our sins but also for our sicknesses. I actually heard a man say that when Jesus was on the cross, he literally experienced every human sickness, from cancer to muscular dystrophy to the common cold. Those who hold this view contend that because Jesus died for our sicknesses, we Christians can be set free from sickness in the same way we are forgiven of sin. Usually the Christian is exhorted to "confess" the sickness and claim the blood of Christ for healing. If symptoms of the sickness persist, that is just Satan trying to get us to fall back into unbelief. If we "name it and claim it," they say, we will be healed.

The biblical basis for the claim of healing in the atonement seems fairly strong. Isaiah predicted seven hundred years before Jesus was born that the suffering servant of the Lord would in some way bear our sicknesses: "Surely he took up our infirmities [literally, our sicknesses] and carried our sorrows [or pains], yet we considered him stricken [a word used of a person who has a terrible disease[1]] by God" (Isaiah 53:4). Then Isaiah adds, "By his wounds we are healed" (v. 5). Fortunately, the Holy Spirit's commentary on this Old Testament prophetic picture can be found in two New Testament passages.

Matthew gives us a general overview of Jesus' healing ministry: "When evening came, many who were demon-possessed were brought to [Jesus], and he drove out the spirits with a word and *healed all the sick.*" Then in his characteristic manner of pointing back to the Hebrew Scriptures as validation for all that Jesus did, Matthew adds: "This was to fulfill what was spoken through the prophet Isaiah: 'He took up our infirmities and carried our diseases' " (Matthew 8:16-17).

What is significant is that Matthew quotes this passage from Isaiah in the context of Jesus' healing ministry, not in the context of Jesus' atoning death on the cross. Jesus, as God's promised Messiah, carried away human sickness by his work of miraculous healing, not by bearing sickness on the cross. Jesus fulfilled Isaiah's prophecy every time a person was healed by his touch or his word.

The apostle Peter quotes Isaiah's prediction that we would be "healed" by Jesus' scourging, but he quotes it as he talks about our *spiritual* healing through salvation: "[Jesus] himself bore our *sins* in his body on the tree, so that we might die to *sins* and live for righteousness; by his wounds you have been healed" (1 Peter 2:24). Nowhere in Scripture are we given any indication that Christ took upon himself human sicknesses in the same way as he did human sin. The apostle Paul clearly says that God the Father "made [Jesus] who had no sin to be *sin* for us" (2 Corinthians 5:21). The Bible never says that Christ was made *sickness* for us.

It is true that Christ's sacrifice on the cross made provision for redeeming us as complete human beings. When we believed, the redemption of our spirits *and* our bodies was secure. Bodily redemption, however, comes at the resurrection. God will not simply prop up the weak, decaying bodies we have now; instead, he will raise us up in new and glorious bodies, suited for eternity (Romans 8:23; Philippians 3:21). Healing *is* in Christ's atonement, but it is that future, forever healing that will come when we are clothed in immortality.

Myth No. 3: "God Wants Every Christian to Be Well"
Closely related to the claim of present physical healing in the atonement is the boast of those who preach a health-and-wealth

gospel—that God wants every believer to be healthy. I sniffled and coughed my way through three morning services one Sunday only to be confronted after the third service by a visitor: "You of all people should know that it is never God's will for any Christian to be sick! Claim your healing! God wants you well."

Believe me, no one *wanted* to be healed more than I did that morning—and God did raise me up. A few days of rest and some medical care were used by a loving Father to restore my health. As I rested and recovered during those days, I thought about what the woman had said to me. I wondered how those words would have sounded to the apostle Paul, suffering from his physical affliction, or to Epaphroditus, sick to the point of death, fighting for his life. I wondered how her words would sound to Job or to a Sudanese Christian too malnourished to withstand the ravages of disease. I wondered how many Christians were suffering in despair because some person had spoken such cruel words of condemnation to them.

We Christians may become sick, and we, like Paul and Epaphroditus and Job and millions of other faithful believers, may come to realize that we are sick within the will and purpose of God. He is the potter, and we are the clay. When the flu lays us low or when we pray for a sick friend, we have to acknowledge the truth of the Bible's analysis of our present condition: "Outwardly we are wasting away" (2 Corinthians 4:16).

Myth No. 4: "Jesus Heals the Same Way Yesterday, Today and Forever"
That "Jesus Christ is the same yesterday and today and forever" is a wonderful truth. In fact, it is a biblical declaration (Hebrews 13:8). Some Christians have interpreted that declaration to mean that since Jesus healed miraculously, instantaneously and immediately while he was on earth (yes-

terday), he should and will heal the same way today.

But is that really what that biblical statement means? I'm certainly not saying that Jesus *can't* heal or do other miracles today like he did during his earthly ministry or that he *won't* at times heal miraculously. But does the declaration in Hebrews require Jesus to work today as he did in the Gospels?

Jesus *is* the same today as he has ever been or ever will be in his character. His nature of grace and love and faithfulness never changes. But there have been many changes in the way Jesus operates in our world or in our lives. For hundreds of years, animal sacrifices were part of God's program for his people, but no one brings an animal sacrifice to church today. God's program changes. The wondrous outpouring of spectacular healings that accompanied Jesus' earthly ministry was designed to validate his claim to be Israel's Messiah. The Bible tells us why the miracles were performed and for what reason. The Scriptures also indicate that after that relatively short period of intense miraculous activity, God's people would enter a time when God would work differently. His nature never changes, but his program is under his sovereign control.

To demand that Jesus *must* heal today exactly as he did in the past is to deny his ability to work in our lives as he alone chooses. Those who claim that all miracles ceased with the apostles face the same problem. We have to be careful here too. To put God in any kind of a theological box is dangerous business. He may just burst through that box in such a dazzling display of power that our lives will never be the same. We seek to know God's ways through what he has revealed in his Word, but we always tread humbly before his awesome presence. The person who thinks he or she has God all figured out hasn't learned the most fundamental thing about him. He is wholly "other," totally unlike us, a sovereign King who reigns in majesty over his creation. Be sure to speak humbly of his glory.

Myth No. 5: "Sin Keeps You from Being Healed"

Job's three friends came to comfort their friend at the deepest point of his loss and pain—and they started so well! They were silent for seven days. Then they began to talk and ruined everything. Each of the three, in varying degrees of brutality and frustration, accused Job of the same thing. They were convinced that Job was sick and suffering because of sin in his life. Eliphaz, Bildad and Zophar had swallowed the line that righteous people don't suffer. Therefore, if Job was suffering (and he was), he must have committed a huge, secret sin. "Just admit your guilt, Job," they said, "and God will restore your health." Job maintained that he had done nothing that deserved such an attack from God.

We have already seen that sickness *may* come into our lives as God's discipline for sin. Job's friends, however, are still around. Their names are different, but they come to a sick Christian with the same accusation: "What have you done to deserve this?" More often, we ask ourselves the same question when serious sickness or tragedy strikes. Gnawing away at our souls is the thought that God is punishing us for some sin in the past.

We should examine our hearts carefully when sickness comes upon us. If we are walking in disobedience in some area, we should confess the sin and make whatever changes God directs us to make. I sometimes encourage sick people to allow the Spirit of God to search their hearts. But I also know as a pastor and from personal experience that we may have a clean heart and clear conscience before God and still be sick. To accuse a fellow believer of continuing sin because he or she continues to be sick is not only unbiblical, it is cruel. Most of the people in the Bible who were sick were not sick because of their own sin. They were faithful followers of Christ who for a variety of reasons in God's wise plan had to endure physical sickness.

The late Joe Bayly knew a lot about sickness and death. He watched three sons die—one at eighteen days old after surgery, another at five years old with leukemia, the third at eighteen years old after a sledding accident. In his little book *The Last Thing We Talk About* Bayly tells a moving story that powerfully summarizes what I have tried to say in this chapter about the easy and trivial answers we can sometimes toss toward those who are sick. A month or so after Joe's five-year-old died of leukemia, a well-meaning Christian told him that his son would not have died if Joe and his wife had possessed enough faith.

"Do you really believe that?" Joe asked.

"Yes, I do," the man replied.

Joe responded, "Do you believe it enough to pray that your own child will become sick with leukemia so that you can prove your faith?"

After a long silence, the man replied, "No, I don't."

Joe concludes with this gentle but pointed (and needed) rebuke:

I do not object to such zealots when they are dealing with other adults. I do object to the traumatic effect they may have on children and teenagers.

The summer after our eighteen-year-old died, our sixteen-year-old daughter was at a Christian camp. A visiting minister, in the presence and with the silent acquiescence of the camp director, told this grieving girl, "Your brother need not have died, if your parents had only had faith for his healing. It is not God's will for one to die before the age of sixty."

When our daughter told us this in a letter, I thought about one who died in His early thirties, one who loved children enough not to hurt them.[2]

Sometimes those Christians who are most zealous for miracles try to take the place of God in other people's lives.

Chapter 9
MIRACLES
OF
DECEPTION

*I*f you ever visit the city of Atlanta, one of the must-see attractions is Atlanta Underground. In the heart of the city, underneath the city streets, are several block of stores, restaurants and shirt shops. Along the broad walkway you will find a variety of musicians, jugglers, palm readers and fortunetellers. On a recent visit to Atlanta, I sat down next to a man who claimed to be able to tell the future and heal any number of emotional and physical diseases. It did not seem like a very busy afternoon, so I asked him if he would answer a few questions. He was a friendly fellow and readily agreed.

I told him that I was working on a book about miracles and asked him if he had ever seen someone healed miraculously. His reply was immediate: "Every day!"

I was more than a little skeptical. "Every day? What exactly happens when these people are healed miraculously?"

He told me that emotional problems are usually cleared up in a few minutes for his twenty-dollar fee. He simply gives people a glimpse into the future and tells them how some problem in their life will be resolved, and they leave with a huge burden of worry lifted from their shoulders.

"How do you know the future?" I asked.

In a refreshing burst of honesty, he said, "Most of the time I just guess. What does it matter? The people feel better, and it costs them less money and less time than an appointment with a therapist." When I pressed him about seeing into the future, he said, "Once in a while I do go into a trance and see the future pretty clearly—but I don't like to do that very often. I feel like someone else takes over my body. It's really pretty scary."

Another category of miracles that the Bible talks about are not the kind that we should pray for or seek. They are, in fact, pretty scary. These are miracles of deception, miracles that come from Satan or from demons. They are usually cloaked in the guise of magic or sorcery or even in the predictions of a fortuneteller or a tarot card reader. Sometimes these "miracles" are not really miracles at all but are deliberate deceptions designed to extract money from gullible customers. But the Bible is also clear that Satan and his forces can, at times, produce real miracles—works of supernatural power not designed to bless those who receive them but to deceive them into false worship.

A Staff Becomes a Serpent

The first example of deceptive miracles in biblical history comes during a time of intense miracles from God. As Moses stood before the Pharaoh of Egypt and demanded the release of the people of Israel from slavery, Pharaoh mocked Moses' God and refused to let Israel go. In a demonstration of the power of the Lord God, Aaron threw the wooden staff of Moses onto the floor of Pharaoh's palace. The staff became a serpent (Exodus 7:10). Actually the word used there can mean any large reptile. Some scholars suggest that it may have been a crocodile (an animal considered sacred in Egypt) or a large lizard. The transformation was an incredible miracle.

Pharaoh, however, was surrounded by an impressive group of wizards and pagan priests. They were able by "their secret arts" to do the same thing Aaron had done. As each one threw down his staff, it became a snake. But the snake from Aaron's staff swallowed up those other snakes in a display of God's mastery over the powers of evil (Exodus 7:11-12).

Later, when Moses struck the water of the Nile River and "changed [it] into blood," the Egyptian magicians again were able to duplicate the miracle (Exodus 7:20-22). They even brought frogs upon the land as Moses did in the second plague (Exodus 8:7). By the time of the third plague on Egypt, however, the magicians and sorcerers had to concede defeat. They tried by their secret arts to produce a plague of gnats as Moses had done but could not. Their testimony to Pharaoh was that this plague was "the finger of God" (vv. 18-19).

We are not told whether the acts of the Egyptian magicians were actual miracles or if they were able to mimic Moses' miracles by trickery and sleight of hand. Whatever the source, their works were certainly *not* from God. The Old Testament writers took an unwavering stand against the occult and any form of magic or sorcery. Perhaps his exposure to the secret arts of the Egyptians prompted Moses to speak such strong prohibitions to Israel:

Let no one be found among you who sacrifices his son or daughter in the fire, who practices divination or sorcery, interprets omens, engages in witchcraft, or casts spells, or who is a medium or spiritist or who consults the dead. Anyone who does these things is detestable to the LORD, and because of these detestable practices the LORD your God will drive out those nations before you. You must be blameless before the LORD your God. (Deuteronomy 18:10-13)

Magic and Fortunetellers

Magic in the days of the New Testament was not a form of entertainment; it was a technique for manipulating supernatural forces to gain one's own desires. When Philip the evangelist came to Samaria to preach the message of Christ, he had to face Simon the sorcerer, a man who had amazed the people of the region with his magic. Simon, however, professed to believe in Christ and was baptized. He followed Philip everywhere, captivated by the great signs and miracles he saw (Acts 8:9-13).

When the apostles Peter and John arrived in Samaria and became the channels through whom the Holy Spirit came upon the Samaritans, Simon was convinced that he had discovered the secret technique of miraculous power. He offered Peter and John money if they would give him the ability to confer the Spirit on people. Peter issued a stunning rebuke: "May your money perish with you, because you thought you could buy the gift of God with money!" (Acts 8:20). Simon the magician (or Simon Magus) became the preeminent example of a heretic in the writings of the early church fathers.

Paul and Barnabas were confronted by a Jewish sorcerer on the island of Cyprus. This false prophet, Bar-Jesus, tried to turn the proconsul of the island, Sergius Paulus, away from faith in Christ. Paul denounced Bar-Jesus as a "child of the devil and an enemy of everything that is right!" (Acts 13:10). He then struck the man with temporary blindness. When the proconsul saw the judgment of God fall on this sorcerer, he believed the message Paul and Barnabas had brought.

In the city of Philippi, Paul encountered a slave girl who "had a spirit by which she predicted the future. She earned a great deal of money for her owners by fortune-telling" (Acts 16:16). When Paul rebuked the evil spirit who possessed her, a riot started. Paul and Silas were beaten and thrown into jail.

It is clear from these biblical accounts that not all miraculous works come from God. The fortuneteller in Philippi and (at times) the palm reader in Atlanta were able to see into the future through the power of a demon. The magical acts of Pharaoh's wizards came from a power greater than themselves. Supernatural acts require a supernatural source of power. Demons are sinful angels who have chosen to rebel against God. But even sinful angels retain their power—a power much greater than human power (2 Peter 2:11). Demons sometimes use the various techniques of those who practice the secret arts of the occult to deceive people.

Christians should have no part in tarot cards or ouija boards or palm reading. I am convinced that most psychics are frauds, but some are channels through which demonic forces seek to lead people away from Christ. Satan's angels and Satan himself will transform themselves into angels of light if they can use that masquerade to deceive people. Demons will try every method to blind people to the gospel and keep them in bondage to things that hinder them from coming to God (2 Corinthians 4:4; 11:14; Galatians 4:8).

The reaction of believers in the New Testament to all forms of occult magic and sorcery was drastic and immediate. In Ephesus, new Christians who had practiced sorcery before their salvation gathered their scrolls together and burned them publicly—at great financial sacrifice but at far greater public testimony to their liberation in Christ (Acts 19:18-20).

All this is not a blanket condemnation of everything that is called "magic" today. Many Christians use magic (also called "illusion") as entertainment or even as the means to present the gospel. They are quick to explain, however, that their tricks are illusions and do not originate from a power outside themselves. The biblical warnings are directed at *occult* magic that was designed to manipulate a supernatural power.

Miracles Outside the Christian Faith

Other religions and many cults claim miraculous works. The practitioners of Christian Science, for example, regularly give testimony to physical healing. Their "healing," however, is based on a denial of sickness, not the presence of God's power. Mary Baker Eddy, the founder of the Christian Science movement, taught that sickness, pain and sin do not really exist—unless we "believe" that they exist. The path to healing, therefore, is to remove such nonexistent entities from the mind. This basic belief of Christian Science is in direct disagreement with the Bible's declaration that sickness and sin are real aspects of the human condition.

The religion of Islam, especially the Sufi orders of the Islamic faith, lays claim to many miracles of healing and supernatural intervention in our world. According to the Qur'an and Muslim tradition, the prophet Muhammad rode his horse, Buraq, through the air one night from Mecca to Jerusalem. He then ascended into heaven in a magnificent miracle from Allah. Sufi martyrs and saints are said to walk on water, fly through the air and communicate directly with animals.

The Hindu god Ganesha, usually depicted with an elephant's head and four arms, is worshiped as the one able to remove all obstacles to financial and spiritual success. Mormons believe that an angel directed the prophet Joseph Smith to golden plates buried in a hillside on which the Book of Mormon had been inscribed.

How should we Christians evaluate the claims of miraculous events that we hear or read about? Obviously, if those claims come from people who reject the truth of the Bible or who refuse to acknowledge Jesus Christ as Lord and Savior, we can either dismiss the miracles as untrue or conclude that they are deceptive miracles designed to draw men and women away from God's true Savior.

But what about reports of miracles from those who claim to be Christians or at least believers in God? Should we simply accept those events as genuine miracles? I am convinced that we need to scrutinize those claims even *more* carefully. The apostle John warns us to "test the spirits," not just trust anyone who claims power in the name of Jesus (1 John 4:1-3).

In the Old Testament, God gave his people a series of tests for evaluating anyone who came to them claiming to be a prophet. If a prophet claimed to speak in the Lord's name but what he predicted did not come to pass, the prophet was to be rejected (Deuteronomy 18:22). But accurately predicting a future event was not enough to verify a prophet's claim. Performing a miracle wasn't enough either! We tend to think that if a person performs a miracle in God's name, the person must be a genuine representative of the Lord. But that's not necessarily true.

Moses warned that a prophet might come to Israel and claim to speak the truth and even perform a miraculous sign or predict a future event. If, however, the prophet said, "Let us follow other gods"—that is, if the prophet did not hold to the truth that God had already revealed in his Word—that prophet was to be rejected. "The LORD your God," Moses explained, "is testing you to find out whether you love him with all your heart and with all your soul" (Deuteronomy 13:1-5).

Jesus issued a similar warning to those who follow him: "Watch out for false prophets. They come to you in sheep's clothing, but inwardly they are ferocious wolves" (Matthew 7:15). Jesus then adds twice that we will recognize the false prophets "by their fruit" (vv. 16, 20). Isn't the "fruit" the miracle itself that is done in Jesus' name, and isn't that sufficient to prove that a man or woman is a true servant of Christ? Not according to Jesus. He goes on in the very next passage to describe a dramatic scene at the final judgment:

Not everyone who says to me, "Lord, Lord," will enter the kingdom of heaven, but only he who does the will of my Father who is in heaven. Many will say to me on that day, "Lord, Lord, did we not *prophesy in your name,* and in your name *drive out demons* and *perform many miracles?"* Then I will tell them plainly, "I never knew you. Away from me, you evildoers!" (Matthew 7:21-23)

On another occasion Jesus told his disciples to exercise great discernment toward those who claim to have knowledge of Christ, because "false Christs and false prophets will appear and *perform great signs and miracles* to deceive even the elect—if that were possible" (Matthew 24:24).

The only sure standard for evaluating the claims of those who announce a ministry that is blessed of God is the clear teaching of God's Word. Jesus said we are to build our lives and ministries on "these words of mine" (Matthew 7:24)—words that "will never pass away" (Matthew 24:35).

The apostle Paul was just as convinced about the importance of evaluating those who claim to teach God's truth or do God's work. He told the Galatian Christians that even if an angel from heaven came to them, they were to measure the angel's words against the yardstick of the gospel. If the angel departed from the truth that Paul had preached, the angel was to be "eternally condemned" (Galatians 1:8). We are not to pass critical, self-righteous judgment on each other (Matthew 7:1-4; Romans 14:13), but we are to be extremely discerning about what we embrace as truth from God (1 Thessalonians 5:21; 1 John 4:1).

A worker of false miracles can always be spotted by his or her denial of the clear teaching of Scripture. Evaluate carefully the claims of the television preacher or the miracle worker who comes to your city on a crusade. If his or her teaching departs from biblical truth, or he or she claims the authority to change biblical truth, stay away. That is true even if they name Christ's name and even if they seem to perform powerful miracles. Moses' words still ring with divine authority in our hearts: "It is the LORD your God you must follow, and him you must revere. Keep his commands and obey him; serve him and hold fast to him" (Deuteronomy 13:4).

According to the apostle Paul, the most dramatic display of deceptive miracles will occur when the man of sin comes on the world scene. "The coming of the lawless one will be in accordance with the work of Satan displayed in all kinds of counterfeit miracles, signs and wonders, and in every sort of evil that deceives those who are perishing" (2 Thessalonians 2:9-10). The apostle John in his vision saw "another beast" rise up who would perform "great and miraculous signs, even causing fire to come down from heaven to earth in full view of men" (Revelation 13:11-13).

All the words used of Jesus' miracles and the miracles that God performed through his people are used of Satan's miracles—signs, wonders and works of power. Satan is a subtle and skilled deceiver; he is an experienced liar (John 8:44; Revelation 12:9). He will use even a miraculous work of power to lead people away from the truth of God.

Deception and the Christian
What disturbs me is not that unbelieving people are following after any claim of miraculous power regardless of the source. We should expect those who reject the gospel to seek to fill the spiritual vacuum in their lives with whatever they can find. What bothers me is to see Christians drawn away into cultic groups or New Age mysticism by the deceptive claims of some charis-

matic leader or the "ancient wisdom" of some bestselling book.

I am regularly surprised (and dismayed) by a Christian who tells me about reading a new book or attending a seminar where the latest spiritual guide dispenses his or her wisdom. Christian bookstores are selling books by Deepak Chopra right beside books by Chuck Swindoll! When someone complains (which I regularly do), the bookstore owner's excuse is that "people are asking" for the New Age material.

But the standard for spiritual truth has not changed. The Bible is the measuring stick. If a book departs from the clear teaching of Scripture (no matter who the author or publisher), red flags and loud alarms should go off in your head. Overactive curiosity about the occult or New Age teaching or some spiritual guru's philosophy can have disastrous effects on your spiritual life. God has given you his Word and the guidance of the Holy Spirit so that you will not be led away from the truth. But he has also given you the responsibility to study the Word and to submit to the Spirit so that your ability to discern between good and evil is sharpened.

A Conquered Enemy
What we have learned in this chapter should not frighten us. Although Satan has great power and can at times mimic God's miraculous works, the power of God is far greater than Satan's. Jesus has already triumphed over all of Satan's forces (Colossians 2:15). Therefore, God's people will triumph in any confrontation with that evil power. The apostle John, who wrote so much about the power of Satan to deceive, is also the one who wrote, "The one who is in you [the Spirit of God] is greater than the one who is in the world [Satan]" (1 John 4:4).

Satan and his demons may incite evil men and women to persecute us as followers of Christ. We may eventually be driven from our churches and our homes. We may even suffer torture and death for Christ. But that is all the world can do to us. Jesus said not to fear those who can only kill the body; instead fear God, who can both kill the body and deliver the spirit to hell (Luke 12:5). We are simply following in a long procession of godly men and women who have suffered incredible persecution for their allegiance to Christ, a procession that leads clear back to Jesus, "the author and perfecter of our faith, who for the joy set before him endured the cross" (Hebrews 12:2).

Chapter 10

WAITING
FOR A
MIRACLE

*J*ob *is a name synonymous with suffering. None of us wants to* go through what Job experienced, but we can't help but admire his courage. Job asked the questions we ask when life caves in around us—Why? Why *me?* Why *now?*—and he puts his questions directly to God. Job was not satisfied with silence. He rejected the easy, pious answers of his friends. He refused to take his sufferings quietly. He took a stand before God and protested in full voice. As Eugene Peterson has put it so well, "He refused to let God off the hook."[1]

We sense as we read the book of Job that Job's story is our story. We suffer in the same ways. We lose our health or suffer the financial setbacks of a layoff. We have to face disruption in our marriage and our family. We stand like Job did at the fresh graves of those we love. We ask the same questions Job did, but we usually aren't brave enough to ask them of God. We hide our doubts in a secret corner of our hearts, where they gnaw away at our faith and poison our spirits.

"Our God is a God of miracles!" We speak the words to others who are in a crisis. We believe those words. We have abundant proof of miraculous activity in his Word and even in our own lives. But when the trial comes in its full fury, and especially when the suffering lingers, we are tempted to wonder if God is really as powerful as we thought he was. We ask, "If God really loves me, why doesn't he do something?"

What can you do until the miracle comes? And what if the miracle *never* comes? Maybe you have prayed for healing and trusted God and have even been anointed by spiritual leaders, but the cancer keeps spreading. You have committed your son to the Lord and passionately prayed for God's intervention, but he continues to willfully pursue a lifestyle that cannot please God. The business debt continues to grow, and your best efforts have not turned it around. Christian counselors and all the bestselling books have not stopped your marriage from crumbling; you and your spouse just keep drifting further and further apart. What now?

I have gleaned four principles from God's Word that we can cling to when no miracle seems to come. I have to admit, however, that I am a little reluctant to write them. I do not want to be like Job's friends and give you the impression that these are pat, easy answers to the problem of suffering. There are no easy answers. Neither do I want you to think that just agreeing with these principles will end your pain or difficulty. These are principles that anchor a person in the full blast of the storm; they do not necessarily bring the storm to an end. Each principle points to a particular aspect of God's character that gives courage and hope. What will stabilize you over the long haul of physical pain or emotional turmoil is not a list of pious phrases. Our rock, our stronghold, our haven of peace is the Lord himself.

God Is Present

The first thing to filter into your mind in the darkness of pain is this: *You are not alone.* God has promised never to leave you as an orphan (Hebrews 13:5). I do not know what pressure you are under as you read this, but I want to assure you that God has not abandoned you. He may have put you in a difficult situation. You may be in the furnace of God's testing. But you never face any test alone.

Not long ago I preached a series of messages on the life and impact of Moses. I was impressed by God's statement to Moses from the burning bush—a statement not about Moses but about God's concern for his people: "I have indeed seen the misery of my people in Egypt. I have heard them crying out because of their slave drivers, and I am concerned about their suffering. So I have come down to rescue them" (Exodus 3:7-8). Then God adds, "The cry of the Israelites has reached me, and I have seen the way the Egyptians are oppressing them. So now, go. I am sending you to Pharaoh to bring my people . . . out" (vv. 9-10).

To the Israelites languishing in Egypt and even to Moses herding sheep in the wilderness, it must have seemed as if God had forgotten his people. They had suffered oppression in Egypt for more than eighty years. But the perception of the people who were suffering was not really what was happening with God. If you are suffering, the words God used of his involvement with Israel—"I have indeed seen. . . . I have heard. . . . I am concerned"—can be applied to you.

Your heart-cries to God have been heard. He is involved in your suffering, and he is touched by your pain. In the days and nights of your deepest trial, when you cannot go on in your own strength, the Lord carries you. He is closer than your spouse or dearest friend; he is closer than your own breath.

God Is Sovereign

A second truth to cling to while you wait for God's deliverance is easy to say but hard to flesh out in real life: *Your pain has a purpose.*

God often asked his prophets to do unusual things. He told Jeremiah, for example, to visit a potter's house and watch the potter at work. "So I went down to the potter's house, and I saw him working at the wheel. But the pot he was shaping from the clay was marred in his hands; so the potter formed it into another pot, shaping it as seemed best to him" (Jeremiah 18:3-4). If you have ever watched a person making pottery, you have seen what Jeremiah saw. The potter takes a lump of clay, puts it on a wheel and spins it. Then with skill and care the potter begins to form whatever he or she has in mind to form. If you remember junior high art class, you know that sometimes the clay doesn't cooperate. The potter is not happy with what is formed, so the artist pushes the clay back into a lump and starts over.

God used Jeremiah's field trip to the potter's house to teach him some theology: "Then the word of the Lord came to me: 'O house of Israel, can I not do with you as this potter does?' declares the LORD. 'Like clay in the hand of the potter, so are you in my hand'" (Jeremiah 18:5-6). The truth that God taught Jeremiah that day is a truth taught all the way through Scripture. God is sovereign over his creation. What that means is that God is in control. He has the right to do what he desires to do, and he will succeed in whatever he determines to do. We do not have too much trouble with that concept when it applies to Old Testament Israel—or to the planets—or to Satan. Where we struggle with this truth is when it applies to *us*.

If you want to see the personal impact of God's sovereignty, read Jeremiah 18:6 with your name inserted: "O [your name], can I not do with you as this potter does? . . . Like clay in the hand of the potter, so are you in my hand." God is over me and over you. He has the right to do with me what he desires, and whatever God determines to accomplish in me he will accomplish.

The apostle Paul proclaimed God's sovereign authority over us in a verse we usually quote to someone else who is suffering, but we need to claim it as our own: "And we know that God causes all things to work together for good to those who love God, to those who are called according to His purpose" (Romans 8:28 NASB). I find the greatest comfort in the first three words of that verse—"And we know." Paul does not say, "And we *hope*" or "we *feel*"; he says that we *know* certain facts to be true. That is what makes this verse so practical.

When the doctor's report is that you have cancer, when you are rushed to the hospital with chest pains, when your child is in a car accident, when your mate dies, you had better *know* some things beyond doubt. If you are going to survive the suffering and pain of this life, you need a sure word from God. The love of friends is wonderful; the concern of other believers is needed and deeply appreciated. But when you are alone, when you lie in bed at night and grief or sorrow or pain or doubt rises up to devour you, you need to know that God is in control, or you will collapse into despair.

We have unshakable confidence in God's ability to make us what he desires us to be. He oversees everything that enters the life of the child of God. He either makes it happen or permits it to happen. Through sorrow and joy, through success and failure, through good times and rough times, God is at work. He uses all the circumstances of life to mold us and hammer us and change us. He causes all things to *work together* for good.

Paul does not say that all things are good; he says they work together for good. He does not say that we will see all things working together for good; he says they *do* work together for good, whether we see it that way or not.

George Pentecost, a well-known preacher of a century ago, was asked to visit a woman who was bitter and angry over some deep trials that had come into her life. Pastor Pentecost tried for some time to talk to her, but with no success. Then he noticed that the woman had a piece of needlework on her lap with the backside up. Pentecost said, "That is a rather ugly piece of needlework. I can't see any pattern or beauty. It's just a meaningless mass of threads and knots."

"You are a rather stupid man," was the woman's response. "You are looking at the backside." Turning the piece over, she showed him a beautiful design.

This gentle pastor then said, "Dear woman, God sees your life with all of its trials like this needlework. He is creating the beautiful design, but you see only the underside."

For too long we have been looking at our lives from the wrong side. We have been trying to make sense out of the knots and loose ends instead of focusing on the pattern God is creating. The image God is weaving in each of our lives is the likeness of his own Son, Jesus Christ. The vessel that will emerge from the potter's hand after all the pushing and pressing and pain of this life is the perfect image of Jesus in me and in you. We will not see the finished project, however, until it's completed. So until then we simply have to trust the One who is at work in our lives.

Dick Adomat saw only the knots and twisted strings of life when his wife, Luby, was diagnosed with leukemia. Dick stood by and watched as brief periods of remission were followed by renewed deterioration. One Friday he was told that his wife would not live through the weekend. Luby could not eat or drink; an intravenous feeding kept her from going into shock.

Early on Sunday morning, Dick was awakened with a powerful sense that something was wrong at the hospital. He resisted the feeling for a while but finally went up to his wife's room. He discovered that the IV needle had become dislodged and his wife was moving rapidly into a dangerous state of shock. When he told the nurse on duty, she said that she had called for a doctor to reinsert the supply needle into Luby's artery but the doctor had not come to the floor yet. Dick returned to his wife's room, called the hospital switchboard and told the operator that a doctor was needed in his wife's ninth-floor room immediately. Within two minutes a doctor arrived and reinserted the IV needle. In three weeks, Luby was able to return home.

In the weeks that followed during what would be her final remission, a friend came to Luby's home and had a Bible study for some of the neighborhood women. As a result of that study, Luby accepted Christ as her Savior. When Luby died a few months later, she found herself absent from this life but present with the Lord.

But the story does not end with Luby's death, because her husband was left behind with four children to rear. The months of Luby's sickness had taken their toll on Dick. He took tranquilizers to make it through the day and sleeping pills to make it through the night, and he compounded their effect by turning to alcohol. He had lost his wife, and now he felt he was losing his job and failing his kids. In his despair, he even planned his own suicide. Then the friend who had organized the Bible study in their home invited Dick to come to church. That Sunday evening, Dick Adomat's life was changed forever. He heard the gospel and by faith received Christ. In time he saw his children come to faith in Christ, and the Lord gave him a new wife, Shirley. Today Dick is a chaplain at the Genesee

County Jail and an elder in our congregation. He serves Christ with joy and enthusiasm.

Luby Adomat's sickness and death seemed like a terrible tragedy—and in one sense they were tragic. But from that tragedy a sovereign God brought glory to himself and eternal blessing to Luby and many others. A God like that can be trusted to work powerfully even in the most desperate of situations.

God Is Faithful
The apostle Paul came to the Lord on three separate occasions in a sustained period of prayer with one specific, burning request: he wanted the Lord to remove a physical affliction. God had given Paul magnificent visions, including a vision of heaven itself. Then, in order to keep Paul humble, God had also allowed Satan to pierce Paul with a sharp stake—a thorn in Paul's flesh (2 Corinthians 12:7).

God permits physical or emotional pain to grip us at times so that we will recognize our absolute dependence on him and so that the pride that rises up within us like a flood will be tamed. God may use failure or sorrow in our lives for that purpose. He may use physical pain or illness or heartache or loneliness to produce in us a broken spirit, a dependent spirit, a recognition of our own weakness.

That is not an easy message to get across to success-oriented, self-sufficient, financially secure Christians. At times it may appear that God is a harsh Father. Paul may have felt that way when the pain from the thorn became unbearable. When the apostle cried to God for relief from the pain, God said, "I will do what you ask, but not in the way *you* think is best. I will not remove the thorn. Instead, I will supply more grace so that you can endure the thorn." That answer stayed with Paul and sustained and supported him through the years of his struggle.

"My grace," Jesus said, "is sufficient for you, for my power is made perfect in weakness" (2 Corinthians 12:8).

Christ's promise to Paul leads us to the third principle to cling to when no miracle comes: *Your suffering will be more than matched by an abundant supply of grace.* The strength of Christ is made glaringly obvious against the backdrop of our weakness and pain. God wins with weak players! God succeeds with people who fail. You may be wrestling right now with some wrenching experience in your life. You may feel like fighting or running or dying. God's grace is available to you, and I can tell you from personal experience that God's help in *any* trial is sufficient to see you through it.

Jody Bowling probably had rheumatic fever as a child, because she later developed rheumatoid arthritis and then life-threatening rheumatoid vasculitis. The combination of the arthritis and the medication she must take to keep the vasculitis in remission has left her bones weak and brittle. Jody can fracture a bone simply by walking across the room. She has spent years confined to a bed, months in the hospital and virtually every day in pain.

When you walk into Jody's hospital room, however, you are greeted with a warm smile. Through all her pain Jody has preserved a sweet spirit of trust in the Lord. Her husband, Bob, could have bailed out of the relationship, but for twenty years he has tenderly cared for his wife. He has modeled sacrificial commitment and humble devotion in the eyes of his children and in the eyes of his church family. I do not want to paint an unrealistic picture. I'm sure there have been difficult days of struggle for Bob and Jody and even times of complaint, but they have refused to cultivate any root of bitterness or resentment. They have learned to draw on the abundant grace God offers to meet each new challenge.

Jody brings a framed Scripture verse with her to the hospital, a verse that takes on greater promise with each new crisis: "I consider that our present sufferings are not worth comparing with the glory that will be revealed in us" (Romans 8:18). Until that future glory comes—or until God chooses to miraculously intervene in her life—Jody Bowling will find abounding grace supplied by a loving Father.

God Is Forever

Jody's verse brings us to the fourth principle to focus on in the long nights of pain or suffering or loss: *Your trial will have an end.* The storm breaking over you now will not last forever. An end to your trial may come quickly. God is more than able to invade your body or your situation in miracle-working power. Physical recovery or a change in your job situation or a restoration of a broken relationship may come gradually as you walk in obedience to God and continue to cry out to him. Or the end of suffering may not come until you stand in Christ's presence. Until God brings an end to your pain or sickness, he calls you to trust him.

We can trust him as a Friend who is closer and more compassionate than any friend on earth. We can rely on his power as our sovereign King who rules in grace and goodness. We can trust him as our faithful Shepherd who will never abandon us even in the darkest valleys of life and death. We can rest the full weight of our grief and sorrow and pain on a loving Father who never sleeps and who never gets tired of hearing our cries to him.

When I was a boy, our family visited some large caverns. The tour group stopped every few steps as the guide pointed out the various formations in the cavern. At one stop I decided to walk on ahead and see what was around the next curve. What I didn't know was that the tour guide was getting ready to turn out the lights in the cave to demonstrate what real darkness was like. When the light went out, I was away from the group, and (like everybody else) I couldn't see a thing. I was ready to let out a panic-stricken scream when I felt a hand on my shoulder and heard my father's familiar voice. He said, "Doug, I'm right here. You don't have to be afraid."

When I am in the black cave of despair or pain or sorrow, that's what I hear. My heavenly Father says, "Doug, I'm right here. You don't have to be afraid." I may still be in the dark, but my heart is secure because I'm in the hands of a faithful Father.

You've found me in my struggle.
You've found me in my pain.
You've found me once again asking you "why?"

But as I bring to you my burdens,
As I bring to you my tears,
There's a look of understanding in your eyes.
You give peace and joy and comfort for my "whys."

Jesus, the lover of my soul.
Jesus, the one who makes me whole.
There is no one like you,
No friend who's quite as true.
Jesus, the lover of my soul..

So I'll bring to you my weakness.
I will bring to you my shame.
I will bring the disappointments of my life.

For you're familiar with my sorrow.
You're familiar with my tears.
You're familiar with my cold and desperate cries.
For on the cross you bore the burdens of this life.

Jesus, the lover of my soul.
Jesus, the one who makes me whole.
There is no one like you,
No friend who's quite as true.
Jesus, the lover of my soul.[2]

Appendix 1
BIBLICAL NATURE MIRACLES

The bush burns	Exodus 3:1-6
Moses' rod becomes a snake, other signs	Exodus 4:1-17
The ten plagues occur	Exodus 7—12
The pillar of fire and cloud lead Israel	Exodus 13:21-22; 14:19-24; 33:9-10; 40:34-38
The Red Sea parts and returns	Exodus 14:21-31
Bitter water is made sweet	Exodus 15:22-27
Manna is provided	Exodus 16:1-5, 14
Quail is provided in the wilderness	Exodus 16:8, 11-13
Water emerges from a rock	Exodus 17:1-7
Aaron's rod blooms	Numbers 17
Balaam's donkey speaks	Numbers 22:20-35
Jordan River is crossed	Joshua 3:7—4:18
Jericho's walls crumble	Joshua 6
The sun seems to stand still	Joshua 10:12-14
Gideon's sacrifice is consumed	Judges 6:19-24
Gideon sets out a fleece	Judges 6:36-40

Manoah's sacrifice is consumed	Judges 13:19-20
Water is provided from the hollow place in Lehi	Judges 15:18-19
Meal and oil are provided	1 Kings 17:8-16
Elijah's sacrifice is consumed	1 Kings 18:20-39
Jordan River is divided twice	2 Kings 2:1-8, 12-14
Elijah is taken to heaven in a in a whirlwind	2 Kings 2:9-11
Brackish water is cleansed	2 Kings 2:19-22
Oil is abundantly provided	2 Kings 4:1-7
Poisonous food is cleansed	2 Kings 4:38-41
An iron axhead floats	2 Kings 6:1-7
The shadow of the sun moves back ten degrees	2 Kings 20:8-11
The visible glory of God descends on the temple	2 Chronicles 5:11-14
Three men are protected in the furnace	Daniel 3:8-30
A man's hand writes on the wall	Daniel 5
Daniel is protected in the lions' den	Daniel 6
Jonah is preserved in the stomach of a great fish	Jonah 1—2
God the Son is miraculously conceived in Mary	Matthew 1:18-25; Luke 1:26-35
Water is turned into wine	John 2:1-11
Fish are miraculously caught, twice	Luke 5:1-11; John 21:1-11
Jesus quiets a storm	Matthew 8:23-27; Mark 4:35-41; Luke 8:22-25
More than 5,000 are fed from a small lunch	Matthew 14:13-21; Mark 6:31-44; Luke 9:10-17; John 6:1-14
Jesus walks on water	Matthew 14:22-33; Mark 6:45-52; John 6:15-21
4,000 people are fed from a few loaves and fish	Matthew 15:32-38; Mark 8:1-9
A coin is found in a fish's mouth	Matthew 17:27
An angel opens prison doors	Acts 5:17-32
Philip is transported by the Spirit of God	Acts 8:39-40

Light from heaven knocks Paul to the ground	Acts 9:1-9
An angel delivers Peter from prison	Acts 12:1-19
An earthquake sets Paul and Silas free	Acts 16:19-34
Paul is protected from the effects of a viper's bite	Acts 28:1-6

Appendix 2
MIRACLES OF JUDGMENT

The flood of Noah's day	Genesis 6:5-7; 8:21
Confusion of languages at Babel	Genesis 11:1-9
Men of Sodom blinded	Genesis 19:9-11
Sodom and Gomorrah destroyed	Genesis 19:15-29
The plagues on Egypt	Exodus 7—12
Nile turned to blood; swarms of frogs; gnats; flies; death of animals; boils; hail; locusts; darkness; death of firstborn	
Judgment on Nadab and Abihu	Leviticus 10:1-7
Fire brought upon Israel	Numbers 11:1-3
Miriam stricken with leprosy	Numbers 12
Korah, family and followers swallowed by earth and consumed by fire	Numbers 16; 26:9-11
The plague of snakes and the bronze snake	Numbers 21:4-9
Philistine idol toppled	1 Samuel 5:1-5
Philistines smitten with tumors	1 Samuel 5:6-12
Judgment on the people of Beth Shemesh	1 Samuel 6:19-21

Pestilence because of David's sin	2 Samuel 24:10-25
Jeroboam's hand shriveled	1 Kings 13:4-6
Drought on Israel in response to Elijah's prayer	1 Kings 17:1; James 5:17
Ahaziah's soldiers consumed by fire, twice	2 Kings 1:9-15
Insolent young men killed by bears	2 Kings 2:23-24
Elisha's servant stricken with leprosy	2 Kings 5:26-27
Blindness, confusion on Aramean army	2 Kings 6:8-23
Sennacherib's army destroyed	2 Kings 19:35; 2 Chronicles 32:21; Isaiah 37:36
Uzziah afflicted with leprosy	2 Chronicles 26:16-21
Nebuchadnezzar loses mind for seven years	Daniel 4
A man's hand writes on the wall	Daniel 5
Jesus curses a fig tree	Matthew 21:17-22; Mark 11:12-14, 20-24
Ananias and Sapphira stricken with death	Acts 5:1-11
Herod Agrippa I judged for pride	Acts 12:20-25
Elymas the sorcerer blinded	Acts 13:4-11

Appendix 3

MIRACLES OF JESUS

The Gospels record thirty-five individual miracles of Jesus. They are listed here in approximate historical order. I have also included the method Jesus used, when recorded, in each of his healing miracles.

Miracle	Scripture Reference	Method Used in Healing
Water turned into wine	John 2:1-11	
Official's son healed in Capernaum	John 4:46-54	Word spoken from a distance
Sick man healed at the pool of Bethesda	John 5:1-9	Spoken word
First miraculous catch of fish	Luke 5:4-11	
Demon-possessed man healed in synagogue	Mark 1:23-26; Luke 4:33-35	Word of command
Peter's mother-in-law-healed	Matthew 8:14-15; Mark 1:30-31; Luke 4:38-39	Jesus touched her hand; fever rebuked
Man with leprosy healed	Matthew 8:2-4; Mark 1:40-42; Luke 5:12-13	Jesus touched him

Paralyzed man healed and forgiven	Matthew 9:2-8; Mark 2:3-12; Luke 5:18-25	Spoken word
Man with a shriveled hand healed	Matthew 12:9-13; Mark 3:1-5; Luke 6:6-10	Spoken word
Roman centurion's servant healed	Matthew 8:5-13; Luke 7:1-10	Word spoken from a distance
Widow's son raised to life	Luke 7:11-15	
Blind, mute, demon-possessed man healed	Matthew 12:22; Luke 11:14	[Not recorded]
Jesus calms a storm	Matthew 8:23-27; Mark 4:37-41; Luke 8:22-25	
Two men from Gadara cleansed	Matthew 8:28-34; Mark 5:1-15; Luke 8:27-35	Word of command
Woman with continual bleeding healed	Matthew 9:20-22; Mark 5:25-29; Luke 8:43-48	Woman touched Jesus' garment
Jairus's daughter raised to life	Matthew 9:18-19, 23-25; Mark 5:22-24, 38-42; Luke 8:41-42, 49-56	
Two blind men healed	Matthew 9:27-31	Jesus touched their eyes
Mute, demon-possessed man healed	Matthew 9:32-33	Word of command
More than 5,000 people fed from small lunch	Matthew 14:15-21; Mark 6:35-44; Luke 9:12-17; John 6:5-13	
Jesus walks on water	Matthew 14:25; Mark 6:48-51; John 6:19-21	
Canaanite woman's daughter healed	Matthew 15:21-28; Mark 7:24-30	Word spoken from a distance
Deaf and mute man healed	Mark 7:31-37	Fingers in ears, spitting and touching tongue, spoken word
4,000 people fed from	Matthew 15:32-38;	

small lunch	Mark 8:1-9	
Blind man at Bethsaida healed	Mark 8:22-29	Spit on eyes, laid hands on eyes
Demon cast out of a boy	Matthew 17:14-18; Mark 9:17-29; Luke 9:38-43	Word of command
Coin in a fish's mouth	Matthew 17:24-27	
Heals the man born blind	John 9:1-41	Jesus made clay, applied to eyes, told to wash
Crippled woman restored	Luke 13:11-13	Laid hands on her
Man with dropsy healed	Luke 14:1-4	Jesus touched him
Lazarus raised to life	John 11:1-44	
Ten men with leprosy healed	Luke 17:11-19	Spoken word
Sight restored to two blind men	Matthew 20:29-34; Mark 10:46-52; Luke 18:35-43	Touched their eyes
Fig tree withered	Matthew 21:18-22; Mark 11:12-14, 20-25	
High priest's servant healed	Luke 22:50-51	Jesus touched him
Another catch of fish	John 21:1-11	

General Statements of Jesus' Miracles

Healings in Capernaum	Matthew 8:16-17; Mark 1:32-34; Luke 4:40-41
Healings at Sea of Galilee	Matthew 12:15-21; Mark 3:7-12; Luke 6:17-19
Healings in Gennesaret	Matthew 14:34-36; Mark 6:53-56
More healings in Galilee	Matthew 4:23-24; 9:35
Healings in the wilderness	Matthew 14:14
Healings on the mountain	Matthew 15:29-31
Healings in the region across the Jordan	Matthew 19:2
Healings in the temple	Matthew 21:14
Healings in response to the inquiry of John the Baptist	Luke 7:21
Healings at Bethsaida	Luke 9:11
Sign miracles at Jerusalem	John 2:23-25

The testimony of Nicodemus to Jesus' miracles	John 3:2
The response of the Jews to Jesus' emotion at Lazarus's tomb	John 11:37
The testimony of Jesus' enemies to his miracles	John 11:47-48
The unbelief of some of the Jews in spite of miraculous signs	John 12:37-41
John's testimony to many other miraculous works not recorded in his Gospel	John 20:30

Sayings of Jesus That Refer to His Miracles

Jesus' response to the Pharisees when they accused him of casting out demons by the power of Satan	Matthew 12:22-37; Mark 3:20-33; Luke 11:14-23
Jesus' teaching to his disciples on the miraculous feedings	Matthew 16:5-12; Mark 8:14-21
Jesus' discourse on the fig tree	Matthew 21:20-22
Jesus' answer to the inquiry from John the Baptist	Matthew 11:2-6; Luke 7:18-23
Woe pronounced on Galilean cities	Matthew 11:20-24; Luke 10:13-15
Jesus' blessing on his disciples	Matthew 13:16-17; Luke 10:23-24
Jesus' message to Herod	Luke 13:32
Jesus' sermon after the sabbath healing at the pool of Bethesda	John 5:19-47
Jesus' presentation of himself as the bread of life	John 6:26-59
Jesus' conversation with the blind man who was healed	John 9:35-41
Jesus' question to those about to stone him	John 10:31-38
Jesus' pointing to his miracles as evidence of his divine mission	John 14:11

Notes

Chapter 1: Searching for a Sign

[1] This story comes from an article in the *Flint Journal* about Kasey (January 8, 1996) and from an interview with Kasey's mother. Kasey was born on December 24, 1979.

[2] This story was reported in the *Flint Journal* (December 28, 1995) by Maggie Jaruzel. Ed and his father, Terry, also appeared as guests on Pat Robertson's television program *The 700 Club.*

[3] My account of Tommy's recovery comes from an article in the *Flint Journal* (May 11, 1995).

[4] *A Course in Miracles*, 3 vols. (Tiburon, Calif.: Foundation for Inner Peace, 1975). Quotations are from pages 1-13.

[5] Dean Halverson, "*A Course in Miracles:* Seeing Yourself as Sinless," *Spiritual Counterfeits Project Journal* 7, no. 1, pp. 18-29. See also "A Course in Miracles/Attitudinal Therapy," in *Encyclopedia of New Age Beliefs,* ed. John Ankerberg and John Weldon (Eugene, Ore.: Harvest House, 1996), pp. 1-16.

[6] These remarks are based on a review of Deepak Chopra's books and an interview of Chopra in *The San Diego Magazine,* November 1978, p. 78. See also Catherine Albanese, "The Magical Staff: Quantum Healing in the New Age," in *Perspectives on the New Age,* ed. James Lewis and J. Gordon Melton (Albany: State University of New York Press, 1992), pp. 68-84.

[7] For a fascinating study of the process of canonization (granting sainthood) within the Catholic Church, see Kenneth Woodward, *Making Saints* (New

York: Touchstone, 1996).

Chapter 2: Should We Expect Miracles Today?

[1] On the basis of Galatians 4:15 and 6:11, many Bible scholars have suggested that Paul was afflicted with an eye ailment. Others have suggested epilepsy or malaria.

[2] It is true that the earlier periods of intense miraculous activity were separated by only four to six hundred years, whereas the current period of relative inactivity has lasted for almost two thousand years. The age in which we live, however, is an age in which God deals with his people differently from the way he did in the "training period" under the law. Those living under the law were being guided to maturity by the constraints of the law. Those of us who live on this side of the cross are given the position of fully mature "sons" of God (Galatians 3:24-25; 4:4-5). During this age we believers are to walk by faith, not by sight.

[3] B. B. Warfield (*Miracles: Yesterday and Today* [reprint Grand Rapids, Mich.: Eerdmans, 1965]) summarizes the century following the apostles: "The writings of the so-called Apostolic Fathers contain no clear and certain allusions to miracle-working or to the exercise of the charismatic gifts, contemporaneous with themselves" (p. 96).

Chapter 3: Wonders in the Natural World

[1] Craig Blomberg has an excellent chapter on the debate surrounding Jesus' miracles in *The Historical Reliability of the Gospels* (Downers Grove, Ill.: InterVarsity Press, 1987), pp. 73ff. See also William Lane Craig, "The Problem of Miracles: A Historical and Philosophical Perspective," in *Gospel Perspectives: The Miracles of Jesus,* ed. David Wenham and Craig Blomberg (Sheffield, U.K.: JSOT Press, 1986), pp. 9-48. Two articles in *Dictionary of Jesus and the Gospels,* ed. Joel B. Green, Scot McKnight and I. Howard Marshall (Downers Grove, Ill.: InterVarsity Press, 1992), are also helpful: Craig Blomberg, "Gospels (Historical Reliability)," pp. 291-97, and B. L. Blackburn, "Miracles and Miracle Stories," pp. 549-60.

[2] Paul Barnett, *Is the New Testament History?* (Ann Arbor, Mich.: Servant/Vine, 1987), p. 116.

[3] C. S. Lewis, *Miracles* (1947; reprint New York: Simon & Schuster, 1996), p. 97; see also *Mere Christianity* (1943; reprint New York: Macmillan, 1971), p. 56.

[4] For a defense of the position that we should see the same level of miraculous activity today that Christians experienced in the early church, see Wayne Grudem, *Systematic Theology* (Grand Rapids, Mich.: Zondervan, 1994), pp. 358-72. See also Gary Greig and Kevin Springer, eds., *The Kingdom and*

the Power (Ventura, Calif.: Regal, 1993).
[5]Harold Remus, "Miracle," in *Encyclopedia of Early Christianity*, ed. Everett Ferguson (New York: Garland, 1990), p. 603.
[6]Corrie ten Boom, with John and Elizabeth Sherrill, *The Hiding Place* (Washington Depot, Conn.: Chosen Books, 1971). This account can be found on pp. 184-85.
[7]Ibid., p. 185.

Chapter 4: Victory over Death
[1]Frank Morison, *Who Moved the Stone?* (reprint Grand Rapids, Mich.: Zondervan, 1992).
[2]I have dealt with the issue of death and what comes after death in the book *After Life: What the Bible Really Says* (Downers Grove, Ill.: InterVarsity Press, 1995).
[3]Betty J. Eadie, *Embraced By the Light* (Placerville, Calif.: Gold Leaf, 1992). For a biblical response to Betty Eadie's book, see my booklet *Deceived By the Light* (Downers Grove, Ill.: InterVarsity Press, 1995). Another excellent analysis of near-death experiences is Richard Abanes, *Journey into the Light: Exploring Near-Death Experiences* (Grand Rapids, Mich.: Baker Book House, 1996).

Chapter 5: Rebuking the Devil
[1]For a study of the biblical teaching on angels, see my book *Angels Around Us* (Downers Grove, Ill.: InterVarsity Press, 1994).
[2]Beelzebub or Beelzeboul comes from the Hebrew name Baal-Zebub ("lord of the flies," see 2 Kings 1:2), which was itself a parody of the phrase *Baal-Zebul* ("exalted Baal"). The name came to be used of Satan.
[3]I am indebted to Wayne Grudem (*Systematic Theology* [Grand Rapids, Mich.: Zondervan, 1995], p. 418) for some of the ideas expressed in this paragraph.
[4]This summary of Chris Kline's experience comes from my personal conversation with her and from her book *A Brilliant Deception* (South Plainfield, N.J.: Bridge, 1991). Her quotation is from page 266.
[5]See Marguerite Shuster's excellent article "Giving the Devil More Than His Due," *Leadership* 12, no. 3 (Summer 1991): 64-67.

Chapter 7: What to Do When You Get Sick
[1]Wayne Grudem, *Systematic Theology* (Grand Rapids, Mich.: Zondervan, 1994), p. 1064.
[2]John H. Armstrong, *A View of Rome: A Guide to Understanding the Beliefs and Practices of Roman Catholics* (Chicago: Moody Press, 1995), p. 67.

Chapter 8: "Do You Have Enough Faith?"
[1]See, for example, 2 Kings 15:5 and Genesis 12:17.
[2]Joseph Bayly, *The Last Thing We Talk About* (Elgin, Ill.: Cook, 1973), p. 88.

Chapter 10: Waiting for a Miracle
[1]Eugene Peterson, *Job: Led By Suffering to the Heart of God* (Colorado Springs, Colo.: NavPress, 1996), p. 5.
[2]This song was written by Perry LaHaie. It is available on his recording *Grace and Mission*, Missio Christus Music, c/o WUGN, P.O. Box 366, Midland, MI 48640; (517) 631-7060. The lyrics are used by permission.

SCRIPTURE INDEX

Genesis
1:31 *93*
5:24 *51*
6:5-7 *26*
8:1 *26*
12:17 *149*
19:14-26 *26*
21:2 *26*
25:8 *51*

Exodus
3:7-10 *128*
3:10 *17*
4:1 *34*
4:1-9 *16, 34*
4:11 *84*
4:30-31 *16*
7:3 *17, 18*
7:10 *117*
7:11-12 *117*
7:17 *17, 18*
7:20-22 *117*
8:7 *117*
8:18-19 *117*
14:21-22 *40*
15:26 *81*
16 *40*
17 *40*
30:30 *100*
31:13 *16*

Numbers
21:4-9 *80*

Deuteronomy
6:22 *18*
11:16-17 *24*
13:4 *123*
18:10-14 *118*

18:22 *121*
26:8 *17*
32:3-4 *84*
32:17 *64*
34:5-6 *51*

Joshua
6 *40*
7 *40*
10 *40*

Judges
6:16-22 *17*

1 Samuel
10:1 *100*
10:10 *100*
16:13 *100*

1 Kings
2:10 *51*
16:29-33 *23*
17:7-16 *41, 49*
17:19-24 *53*
17:21 *54*
18:19-39 *40, 64*

2 Kings
1:2 *149*
2:11 *51*
4:32-37 *53*
4:34-35 *54*
5:1-14 *80*
6:1-6 *41*
13:20 *51*
13:20-21 *53*
15:5 *149*
20:4-6 *95*

2 Chronicles
16:12 *94*
26:19-21 *26, 88*
32:20-22 *26*

Job
1—2 *85-86*

7:6 *84*
12:23 *19*

Psalms
22:28 *19*
24:1 *93*
34:4 *87*
66:5-6 *40*
73:26 *104*
73:28 *104*
91:1 *21*
106:9 *40*
106:37-38 *64*
135:9 *18*
136:10-15 *40*

Isaiah
35:5-6 *35*
37:36 *26*
51:10 *40*
53:4-5 *109*
63:11-13 *40*

Jeremiah
10:12 *18*
18:3-6 *129, 130*

Daniel
3 *39*
4:17 *19*

Matthew
4:1-11 *68*
4:23-24 *80*
6:7 *92-93*
7:1-4 *122*
7:7 *93*
7:15-16 *121*
7:20 *121*
7:21-23 *122*
7:24 *122*
8:16 *65, 78*
8:16-17 *80, 109-10*
8:27 *17*
9:8 *37*
9:18-25 *53*

9:24 *55*
9:36 *36*
10:7-8 *68*
11:2-4 *35*
11:2-6 *43*
11:18 *65*
11:20 *18*
12:22 *65, 67*
12:24 *43, 67*
12:25-26 *67*
12:28 *43, 65, 68*
12:40 *44*
12:43-45 *77*
13:58 *18, 108*
14:14 *36*
14:15-20 *41*
15:32-38 *41*
17:14-16 *47*
17:20 *47, 78*
19:3-6 *43*
20:30-34 *36*
21:21-22 *47*
24:24 *122*
24:35 *122*
25:41 *62, 71*

Mark
1:21-27 *65*
1:23 *66*
1:29-34 *67*
1:32-34 *67*
1:34 *65*
3:10-12 *80*
3:15 *68*
3:30 *43*
4:41 *17*
5:9-13 *78*
5:15-16 *65*
5:20 *17*
5:39 *55*
5:41 *54*
5:42 *53*
6:5-6 *48, 108*
6:47-51 *41*
9:29 *74, 78*
14:36-39 *92*

Luke
1:35 *18*
2:12 *16*
4:25 *44*
4:27 *44*
4:33 *66*
5:20 *107*
6:17-18 *80*
6:18 *65*
7:11-15 *53, 108*
7:13 *36*
7:16 *53*
7:21 *80*
8:22-25 *41*
8:25 *17*
8:26-39 *108*
8:30 *65*
8:30-33 *78*
8:43-44 *95*
8:43-48 *107*
8:50 *107*
8:52 *55*
8:55 *56*
9:39 *65*
10:17 *68*
10:18 *69*
10:20 *78*
11:11-13 *108*
11:14-16 *43*
12:5 *125*
13:10-17 *108*
13:32 *80*
16:31 *48, 60*
17:26-27 *43*
17:28-29 *43*
20:37 *43*

John
2:1-11 *41*
2:7-11 *16*
3:2 *35*
5:1-13 *108*
6:49 *43*
8:44 *123*
9:1-16 *16*
9:2-3 *87*

10:25 *43*
11:1-44 *53*
11:4 *87*
11:11-14 *56*
11:43 *54*
11:43-48 *16*
11:45 *54*
11:57 *54*
12:10-11 *54*
14:11-12 *31*
17:15 *76*
20:30-31 *36*

Acts
2:22 *18, 35, 43*
2:31-32 *57*
2:41 *43*
3:9-10 *81*
3:16 *81*
4:30 *18, 81*
5:1-11 *88*
5:12 *18, 27, 69*
5:16 *27, 69*
8:5-8 *69*
8:6 *35*
8:6-7 *27*
8:9-13 *118*
8:20 *118*
9:32-35 *36*
9:36-42 *36, 53*
9:40-41 *54*
12:1-19 *27*
13:10 *118*
14:8-10 *27*
16:16 *119*
16:16-18 *27, 69*
19:11-12 *28*
19:18-20 *119*
20:7-12 *53*
20:10 *54*
28:3-5 *28*
28:7-10 *28*

Romans
1:4 *18, 58*
1:16 *33, 60*

4:11 *16*
4:25 *58*
5:12 *84*
8:18 *135*
8:21 *82*
8:23 *110*
8:29 *58*
8:28 *130-31*
14:13 *122*
16:19 *78*
16:20 *78*

1 Corinthians
1:10 *75*
3:1-4 *75*
10:19-20 *64*
11:30 *88*
12:7-9 *29*
12:9 *29*
12:28 *29*
12:30 *29*
14:20 *78*
15:1-4 *58*
15:1-28 *56*

2 Corinthians
1:21-22 *101*
4:4 *119*
4:16 *111*
5:8 *59*
5:21 *110*
11:14 *64, 119*
12:7 *133*
12:7-9 *29*
12:8 *92, 134*
12:9 *84*
12:12 *17, 18*

Galatians
1:8 *122*
3:24-25 *148*
4:4-5 *148*
4:5 *147*

4:8 *119*
4:13-14 *28*
6:11 *147*

Ephesians
1:19-20 *57*
6:11-12 *72*
6:17-18 *74*

Philippians
1:23 *59*
1:28 *70*
2:9-11 *70*
2:25-30 *29, 82*
3:10 *18*
3:21 *58, 110*
4:8 *78*

Colossians
1:13 *70*
2:15 *70, 124*
4:2 *93*

1 Thessalonians
1:10 *51*
4:14-17 *56, 59*
4:17 *51*
5:18 *21*
5:21 *122*

2 Thessalonians
2:9-10 *123*
3:3 *76*

1 Timothy
5:23 *29, 82, 95*

2 Timothy
4:20 *29*

Hebrews
1:3 *19*
2:3-4 *35*

2:4 *18*
2:14 *70*
9:27 *84*
11:5 *51*
11:6 *107*
12:2 *125*
12:6 *89*
13:5 *128*
13:8 *111*

James
1:6-7 *107*
2:26 *56*
4:2 *91*
4:7 *73*
5:14-16 *28, 99*
5:15-16 *88, 103*

1 Peter
2:24 *110*
5:9 *74*

2 Peter
2:10-11 *75*
2:11 *119*

1 John
2:20 *101*
4:1 *122*
4:1-3 *121*
4:4 *70, 124*
5:18 *76*

Jude
9-10 *75*

Revelation
12:7-12 *69*
12:9 *123*
13:11-13 *123*
20:10 *71*

SUBJECT INDEX

angels 62-63, 64
anointing 28, 31, 88, 98-103
Augustine 46

Chopra, Deepak 14, 124
Christian Science 120
A Course in Miracles 13-14
critical approach to miracles 41-42

death 84
  biblical definition of 56
demons 63-78
  casting out 73, 77-78
disabilities, birth defects 83

Eadie, Betty 60-61

Epaphroditus 29, 82

faith and healing 106-9

healing and the atonement 109-10

Jesus' testimony to his own miracles 43
Jesus' testimony to Old Testament miracles 43-44
Job 85-86, 113, 126-27

magic 118, 119
man of sin 123
Mary, visions of 15
medical care 93
miracle, definition of 18-19
Morison, Frank 50-51

near-death experiences 60-61

occult, sorcery 117, 119, 124

periods of intense miraculous activity 22-28, 40-41
prayer of faith 101-2
providence of God 19-21
purpose of miracles 33-37

reliability of biblical record 42-43
resurrection
  of believer 58-59
  of Jesus 56-58, 61

sainthood 15
Satan 67-68, 70-71, 85-86
sickness and sin 88, 96-98, 113

ten Boom, Corrie 48-49
thorn in the flesh, Paul's 29, 86, 92, 133
Timothy 29, 83, 95

Who Moved the Stone? 51